North Island Designs 4

16 New Patterns from Talented Maine Designers

North Island Designs

North Island Designs 4

16 New Patterns from Talented Maine Designers

By Chellie Pingree
Photos by Peter Ralston

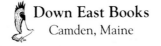

Down East Books
Camden, Maine

ISBN 0-89272-318-1

Photography by Peter Ralston
Graphics and text design by Louis Carrier
Cover design and production consultants: Michael Mahan Graphics
Technical knitting editing by Brenda Sandner
Editing by Helen Popp
Color separations by Vision Graphics

Printed and bound in Hong Kong through Four Colour Imports

10   9   8   7   6   5   4   3   2   1

Down East Books, Camden, Maine

Contents

Welcome

North Island Designs is a business run from an island with a winter population of 350. We produce knitting kits and pattern books and also sell yarns and knitting accessories through our catalogue. There are about eight women who work at the business, and you may have talked with many of us over the years when calling to place an order or ask a knitting question. We all live on the island, and when we need to leave we take an hour-long ride on a nine-car ferry that serves as our link to the mainland. Our children attend the sixty-five-student school here in the community.

This is our fourth knitting book and something of a departure from our previous publications. Over the past year we have had the opportunity to get to know many freelance designers and have included some of their work in our catalogues. This book gives us an opportunity to publish some of their patterns and to include profiles of these wonderful women.

While doing this book, I have had the good fortune to interview twelve women who live in Maine and who consider the art, craft, or business of knitting to be an essential part of their lives. Our conversations were windows through which I could view their creative processes; something vital to all of us whether we work on the assembly line or paint great masterpieces. Listening to them, I began to understand that the appeal of creativity involves the pleasure and challenge of producing something that requires all of one's concentration and focus. For some people, this can be planting a garden or building a house; for a knitter, it can be as simple as constructing a pair of socks or as complicated as designing an intricate product that features ancient and traditional patterns.

In recent history, knitting has been predominantly a women's domain and has served as a very available means of creative expression. It can be picked up and set down as the day's interruptions require. In this way, knitting is an act suited to a woman's life and it is often a way for the knitter to be present in their own world and thoughts for a moment in the midst of the chaos and turmoil of everyday life. Many women described knitting as a way to handle the boredom of waiting for children at the dentist or to create an island of their own during a busy commute, whether on a crowded ferry or a downtown subway.

Susie Hanson said knitting made her feel "close to her grandmother again," and several other women discussed the connection to long-gone family members who knit in their presence or taught them to knit. Many valued the memories of time spent at a relative's side, learning the basic stitch. Others mentioned a more symbolic connection to women of all times who knit as their creative outlet.

All of the knitters in this book have found ways to use knitting to make contributions to their economic well being. The group ranges from Nan Haddon, who runs a very successful sweater company, to my old friend Marion, who knit socks for her family and to sell in our store, to Carol Loehr, who concentrates her efforts on the sheep that produce the raw material essential to great knitting — wool. Many of these women cherish the opportunity to be paid while doing something that they love.

For me, a knitting business provides tremendous challenges and an opportunity to touch the lives of many — those of you who buy our books and kits, the designers who work with us, and my talented coworkers who come in each day to keep our company alive. To all of you connected in one way or another to knitting — our customers and readers and those wonderful women who opened up a piece of their lives and allowed me to include them in this book — many thanks. It has been a privilege.

7

7

Before You Begin
Knitting These Patterns...

Here are a few of our suggestions for getting these knitting projects to come out right.

GAUGE

We cannot stress strongly enough the importance of gauge. It is a simple process that is well worth the time invested. All sweaters are designed to be knit with a certain number of stitches to the inch, and this is far more important than the suggested needle size. The most important step is that you choose the size of needles that will allow you to achieve the required number of stitches to the inch.

To do this, knit a small swatch about 20 stitches wide by three inches high using the main color and the larger of the suggested needles. When you are done, gently press with a damp cloth, then let it cool. Now, measure two inches across and count the stitches; divide this number by two, and you've got your gauge. If you have fewer stitches per inch than the gauge given in the pattern, decrease the size of your needles; if too many, increase the size of your needles, and knit a swatch again. This step is very important to achieve the garment you want, no matter how many years you have been knitting.

Figuring out what size to make is a very logical process. Begin by finding a sweater that fits the way you (or your sweater recipient) would really like a sweater to fit. Then measure the chest, sleeve length, length of the sweater, etc. Here is where the stitch gauge becomes important. If you want your sweater to measure 28 inches around the chest and there are 5 stitches per inch with the type of yarn you are using, you will need approximately 70 stitches each for the front

and back, along with a couple of extra stitches for the seams. Check the pattern to see what size gives that number of stitches across the back.

RIBBING

When you are casting on the lower edge, remember that the ribbing is intended to be elastic as the garment is worn. If you have a tendency to cast on too tightly, use a larger needle to cast on the stitches. Also, remember to bind off neck stitches loosely so that the ribbing can stretch to go over the head.

MULTICOLORED KNITTING

Knitting with two or more colors is very easy, and if you have never done it before, now is a perfect time to start. Knit a small swatch to practice and you will be surprised how simple it is.

When knitting with two colors, don't tie a new color on until you have knit a few stitches with it — then go back and make a simple knot. If you can weave the end in without making a knot at all, so much the better; but often, if you don't attach it somehow, the stitches will have a tendency to loosen up. When you are carrying colors, it is important to carry the unused color for no more than 3 or 4 stitches before twisting the yarns together. If you carry it farther without twisting, you will end up with long strands on the inside that could catch when you put on the sweater.

The intarsia method will be referred to in some of the patterns in this book. This means to use separate strands or bobbins of yarn for each color area, instead of carrying all the different colors of yarn across the

Before you begin...

entire row. You may want to attach more than one ball of main color yarn in some areas. This way the design will lie flat and not pucker. You will be left with ends to weave in, but try to relax and enjoy it - a nice sweater takes times to complete.

Mistakes in multicolored knitting can be corrected by working the correct color in duplicate stitch (page 9) after the garment is complete. Duplicate stitch is also useful in areas where only a small amount of color is called for. A color out of place here or there won't make a great difference.

When near the end of a ball of yarn it is best to start a new ball at the beginning of the next row. To determine if there is enough yarn left on the present ball to make it through another row, figure 1 inch per stitch.

**PUTTING YOUR
SWEATER TOGETHER**

When all the pieces have been finished, be sure to press (block) them before sewing them together. To sew the seams, put the right sides together, taking a straight needle (about a number 5) and use it as a large pin to hold the pieces while backstitching them together. Sew the shoulders first (unless the pattern has called for knitting them to-gether), then the neck ribbing, the side seams and the sleeve seams. Last of all, with the body wrong side out, insert the sleeve, right sides together, and match the seams at the underarms. After the sleeve cap is fitted, backstitch it in place, and press your seams.

Knitted Seam Method: Place shoulder stitches back onto needles from stitch holders. Hold needles together with right sides of fabric touching each other. Then, using a third needle (same size as used for the main part of sweater), insert it through the first stitch of both needles and knit together. Repeat for next stitch on both needles. Then pass first stitch on right needle over second to bind off. Repeat procedure until all stitches are bound off.

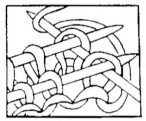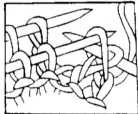

Knitted Seam Method

Backstitch: With right sides of work facing each other line up ends. Working on wrong side, close to edge, follow chart. Stitches should be about 1 knitted stitch in size (2 stitches forward, 1 stitch back).

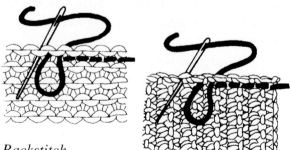

Backstitch

Embroidery

A few embroidery stitches can make a great addition to a sweater - a spark of color as well as texture, a way to make a garment unique. Here is an explanation of the simple stitches we included in some of the patterns in this book.

FRENCH KNOT

This is the perfect stitch for little round designs like apples or flowers in a field. Bring the yarn up through the sweater where you want the knot to be and wind the yarn around the needle 3 to 5 times, close to the sweater. Then insert the needle close by and, holding the twisted yarn with your thumb, pull the needle gently all the way through to form a knot.

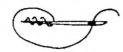

DUPLICATE STITCH

Use this stitch to correct a mistake or to add a stitch in another color after the sweater is complete. Pull the needle up through the stitch below the one to be covered. Pass the needle under both sides of the stitch above the one to be covered and back down through the first stitch.

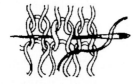

LOOP STITCH

Bring the yarn up through the sweater to form a loop and insert the needle close to the same spot. Then bring the needle back up to catch the other end of the loop.

OUTLINE STITCH

This is somewhat like a backstitch (see page 8) except that each stitch starts just beside and behind the end of the previous stitch, creating a heavier line.

SATIN STITCH

Long and short stitch is a popular stitch for shading areas in a design. The stitch is worked very similar to the back stitch, but there is more color blending. Each stitch from the second row onward pierces the stitch right above it in the preceding row.

Glossary of Terms

approx	approximately
beg	beginning
CC	contrast color
cn	cable needle
co	cast on
dec	decrease, decreases
dp	double pointed
eor	every other row
inc	increase, increases
k	knit
k2 tog	knit 2 together
MC	main color
p	purl
PSSO	pass slipped stitch over
rem	remaining
rep	repeat
rnd	round
RS	right side
rw, rws	row
sl	slip
ssk	slip 2 knit together
st	stitch
St st	stockinette stitch
tw	twist
WS	wrong side
yo	yarn over

Mary Eaton Lee

Mary Eaton Lee came upon knitting as a career later in life, but she certainly wasn't sitting around waiting for it. At 61, Mary has had an intriguing and diverse life. Although in her past she taught carpentry, and administrated a mental health clinic, it was Mary's and her husband's involvement with the sea that eventually brought her to the Maine islands. Her husband is a captain and runs the ferry between Islesboro and the mainland, and Mary, when they arrived ten years ago, worked as the first woman able seaman on the run. No longer a regular on the Islesboro ferry, Mary is occasionally called in the night for an emergency run to deliver a laboring mother or person with a medical problem to the mainland.

This was not their first venture with boats. Years ago, they owned a small freighter and ran cargo between Miami and such exotic places as Port of Spain, Trinidad, and the Caribbean Islands. Mary was the first mate, and her husband the captain. They hauled cars, salt, lumber, and refrigerated cargo, learning the customs and businesses of the countries they traveled to. Today Mary's life is less water and boats than colors and textures and designs.

Mary learned to knit from her mother when she was six. Her mother knit cable stitch sweaters and colorful sweaters for her husband and children. After Mary graduated from knit squares, her first project was a navy blue sweater with garter stitch sleeves for her father. Not only did the sweater fit, but her father cherished it. "It lasted for years, and he wore it like a badge." Such a success would have to be an encouraging beginning for any young knitter. From then on, she always knit, mostly for her three children as they were growing up.

It wasn't until she moved to the island that knitting began to take over. To begin with, all islands have career limitations — you can't travel away to work every day, and often you must create your own niche within the geographical bounds of the community. Mary also found that she was so involved with knitting as a hobby that it was becoming expensive. She decided to invest $500 in a yarn shop and began making sweaters to sell. The next summer, she opened a shop in her house and began selling sweaters of her own design along with traditional guernseys.

It didn't take long for her work to become popular with the summer visitors, and she now knits 25 or more sweaters a year and sells them for $225 and up. Her unique designs depict island scenes or just combine wonderful colors and textures.

Mary's father was an engineer, and she feels that a little of his skills and outlook are in her. As she says, "I love to put things together," and she thinks through exactly how to do a new project before she begins. She can think of her projects in three dimensions and is always looking for innovative ways to build the garment, ways that seem logical to her. Mary also works in cloth, creating quilted jackets, and she is not afraid to transfer skills from one craft to another. She often knits cardigan sweaters in the round and cuts the sleeve and front openings.

Mary is a master sweater builder, whose ability to construct a garment with a fine eye for color, balance, and texture is evident. She is fascinated by color and her memory for color is so good that she can see a shade she favors and find an exact match in a yarn or thread much later. She can knit a sweater with only a photo as a guide or can observe a garment she likes and go home and recreate an exact replica. She loves to work with all yarns, although wool/mohair blends are her favorites. One thing she doesn't like to do is repeat the same design over and over, something which customers often request. She resists, preferring to have each item unique.

What role has creativity played in her life? Knitting has been with her all of her years, and has to be one of the reasons that

she has "never been bored." It has helped her through those years when hours were spent waiting for her kids at the dentist, and it has provided her with an extremely creative outlet while living in an island community of 500. Although at times Mary wishes she had a formal art school background, her venture into the creativity of knitting has taught her many of the rules of art and design. She has learned much through her experiences with needles and yarn and we all benefit as she applies those lessons to crafting beautiful creations.

```
┌─────────┐
│ ▦▦▦▦    │
│ 12      │
│ ▦▦▦▦    │
└─────────┘
```

Geranium Vest

Sizes: Small, Medium, Large

Needles: Sizes 3 and 5 or whatever size needed to obtain stitch gauge of 5 sts and 7.5 rows = 1 inch on larger needles. 1 set size 3 double pointed needles or 16" round size 3.

Materials: Sweater is knitted in knitting worsted weight wool.
2 (3,3) 4 oz skeins of white (MC)
1 oz green for grass
1 oz blue for water
1 oz purple for hills
1 oz light blue for sky
clouds are main color

Embroidery - Done with single strand needlepoint wool.
12 yards dark green for trees and leaves
6 yards medium pink for geraniums
6 yards medium light pink for geraniums
6 yards light pink for geraniums

NOTES
This sweater is knitted in several directions. The middle panel is knitted first, the sides second, the ribbing at the bottom third and finally the armhole and neck finishing. See Diagram A.

STITCHES AND PATTERNS USED
Stockinette Stitch - knit on right side, purl on wrong side.
Seed Stitch - on an odd number of stitches
Row 1 (RS) k1, p1, ending row with k1.
Row 2 (WS) k1, p1, end row with k1.
Every knit stitch is placed above a purl stitch.
Border Pattern - (8 Rows) knit 2 rows (1 ridge). K1, p1 in rib for 4 rows. Knit 2 rows (1 ridge).
Twisted Rib - K1 in the back of the stitch, p1.

Diagram A

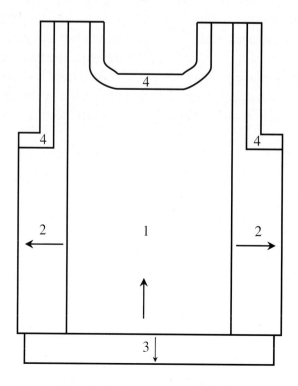

FRONT:

Using larger needles CO 61 sts in white.
Work 8 rws of border pattern. Work in seed
stitch for $1\frac{1}{2}$ (2, $2\frac{1}{2}$) inches. Work 6 rows
of border pattern. Now make the picture.
(See diagram B - 58 rows) Returning to
white yarn work, 6 rws of border pattern.
Work in seed stitch 1($1\frac{1}{4}$, $1\frac{1}{2}$) inches.

SHAPE NECK:

Continuing in seed stitch, work across 18
sts. Put on stitch holder or strand. Bind off
center 25 sts. Work remaining 18 sts.
Continue on these 18 sts for left side decreasing one stitch at neck edge every other
row three times. There are now 15 sts on

Diagram B

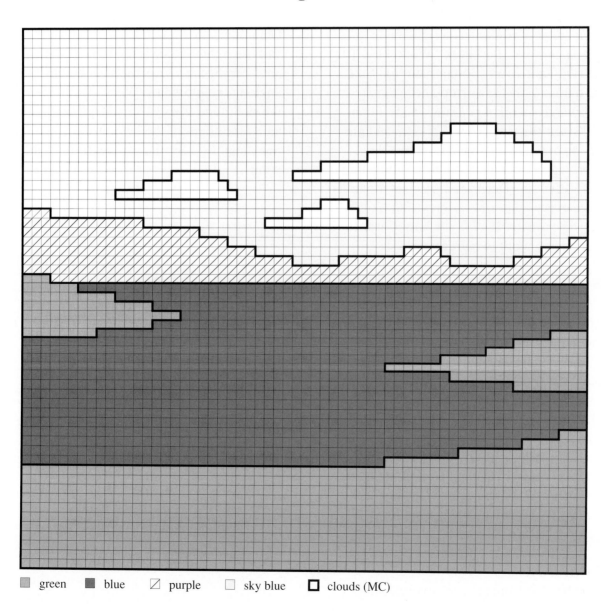

green   ▨ blue   ⧄ purple   ☐ sky blue   ◻ clouds (MC)

Geranium Vest

the needle. Continue working in seed stitch until $3\frac{1}{2}$ (4,$4\frac{1}{2}$) inches above bound off neck stitches. Work 8 rws of border pattern. Cast off. Work right side to correspond.

SIDES
(See diagram A)

<u>Right Side</u> - With the right side of the work facing you, starting at the top, pick up 95 (103,111) sts along the side top to bottom. You are now working at a right angle to previous work. Purl back. Work 4 rws k1, p1 rib. Knit 2 rws (Border pattern). Size medium - work 2 rws stockinette stitch. Size large - work 4 rws stockinette stitch. All sizes knit across 43(47,51) sts and put on stitch holder or strand of yarn. Now working in stockinette stitch on remaining 52(56,60) sts. Decrease 1 stitch at armhole edge every other row 4 times - 39(43,47) sts. Work even 1($1\frac{1}{2}$,2) inches. Cast off. <u>Left side</u> - Work to correspond.

BOTTOM RIBBING
With smaller needles, pick up along the bottom of piece 97(105,113) sts. Work in twisted rib $2\frac{1}{2}$ (3,$3\frac{1}{2}$) inches. Cast off loosely. (The length of the sweater is easily adjusted here.)

BACK
Make the same as the front except no picture panel. Knit that area in stockinette stitch - 58 rows. Count them. Also, do not shape neck. Simply work up to shoulder ending with border pattern all the way across and cast off.

FINISHING
Join back to front at shoulders matching pattern stitch for stitch. Join side seams. *Neck:* with double pointed needles, pick up 98(106,114) sts. Work in border pattern. Cast off. *Armholes:* with double pointed needles, pick up 118(124,130) sts. Work in border pattern. Cast off.

EMBROIDERY
Stitches used are French Knots, Loop Stitch and Outline Stitch. The stems are Outline Stitch. The leaves are Loop Stitch. The Geraniums are French Knots. Crowd them and use lighter color at the top. The trees are Loop Stitch. Vary the size, height and angle of the blossoms. Vary the direction of the stems and trees. Use an Outline Stitch along the edges of the land, water and hills. See diagram C for the general form of the plants.

Diagram C

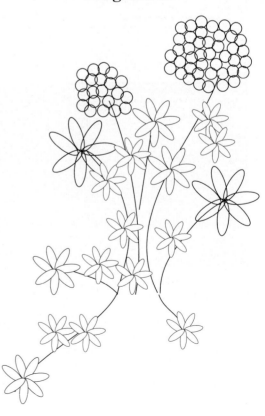

Geranium Vest

Triangle

To make this sweater, I collected sixteen worsted weight yarns, light and dark, which looked well together. Because I have a large collection of leftovers, I was able to make this sweater without purchasing more yarns. Look over what you have, put those you like together, beg from friends, or buy. You will need about 50 ounces, which will be too much but that can not be helped since there are choices to be made along the way and you will use more of some colors than others. The yarns in my sweater are wool and wool and mohair blend. Use anything that pleases you. Wool, mohair, silk, cotton, linen, rayon etc. They all work well together. The more variety of color and texture the more unusual and beautiful your sweater will be. Be daring and try something new and different.

Sizes: 36(38), 40(42), 44(46)
Needles: 1 set straight needles size 7 or
   whatever size needed to obtain stitch
   gauge in pattern stitch of 5 sts = 1",
   5 rows = 1"
   1 set double pointed size 4 needles.
   1 24" or 29" size 4 circular needle.
Materials: approximately 50 ounces worsted
   weight yarn in varying colors - at least 2
   ounces of each color. 4 ounces should
   be a neutral background color for bottom, neck and cuffs.

FRONT
On straight needles cast on 96(102,114) sts in neutral background color. Work 4 rows. Now start colored pattern and work until piece measures 21(23,25) inches. Now in neutral background color only work 4 rows ending on RS.

SHAPE NECK
Knit across 36(38,42) sts and put these on a holder. Cast off center 24(26,30) sts for neck opening. Knit across last 36(38,42) sts. Working on these only, dec 1 st at neck edge eor 4 times. Work 2 rows even. Cast off. Work other side of neck to correspond.

BACK
Work as for front but do not form neck opening. Match front pattern colors.

SLEEVE
On straight needles, cast on 66(72,78) sts in neutral background color. Work 4 rows. Now working in color pattern, increase 1 stitch at each side every inch 15(17,18) times 96(106,114) sts adding color pattern as needed. Work even until sleeve measures 19(20,21) inches or desired length to underarm. Make other sleeve to match. The color pattern can be the same or different, as you choose.

FINISHING
Sew shoulders together stitch for stitch. Sew sleeves to body. Sew underarms and side seams matching color pattern. ***Bottom Facing:*** Along the bottom with circular needle using neutral background color pick up about 192(204,228) stitches. Purl 1 row to turn the facing. Knit 3 rows. Change to another color and knit in stripes of color until facing measures about $3\frac{1}{2}$ inches. Cast off. Sew facing in place. ***Cuff Facing:*** Along sleeve edge with double pointed needles, using neutral background color, pick up about 66(72,78) stitches. Continue as for bottom facing. ***Neck:*** Around the neck edge with double pointed needles, using neutral background color, pick up about 63(67,73) stitches. Knit even for $1\frac{1}{4}$ inches. P 1 row to turn the facing. Knit even for $1\frac{1}{4}$ inches in colored stripes. Cast off and sew in place.

Starting with one light and one dark color, work the first 5 rows. Change to another light and another dark color and work another 5 rows. Change colors every 5 rows varying the direction of the triangles as shown below.

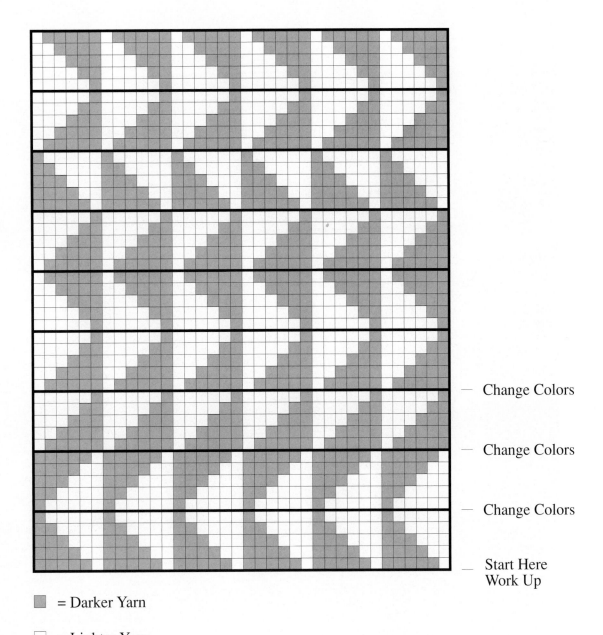

— Change Colors

— Change Colors

— Change Colors

— Start Here
   Work Up

⬛ = Darker Yarn

☐ = Lighter Yarn

Knit on right side and purl on wrong side twisting yarns on the wrong side as necessary.

Triangle

Robin Hansen

After we met, Robin and I were discussing her mitten research and the wonderful museums in Nova Scotia she had visited during a "mitten vacation" while she was seeking out traditional knitting patterns. One of her favorite museums had held a "mitten day," where people brought in their favorite mittens and participated in lively discussions about the origins of these essential winter handwarmers. To Robin, all of this reflected a culture that "cares about the things that matter." When I asked her what that was, she answered, "Folk life."

Robin is less a designer than a preserver of the information that has been passed down over the years through knitting. Author of three popular books on the subject of mittens, along with numerous articles, Robin says her primary interest is in folklore — those facts which are passed down through a culture, usually without the assistance of the written word. Most likely, Robin is the only person in Maine, and perhaps the country, to have written a dissertation on knitting for her doctoral program in Folklore. Doctor Knitting?

The following is an article by Robin describing yet another mitten tradition once very popular with Maine Fishermen.

Maine fishermen's mittens, knitted of white wool, extra large, shrunken and fulled by the fishermen themselves, and worn wet! It sounds unlikely, doesn't it? A fisherman's story. But it's true. Until twenty years ago, most Maine fishermen wore them — wetted down in the cold salt water and wrung out. At the end of the day, their hands emerged from them steaming warm and pink. Are they a local invention? Something from our English ancestors? In fact, they were once worn by fishermen and woodsmen alike throughout the chillier parts of the North Atlantic from Norway to Newfoundland to Rhode Island — and as far away as Seattle and British Columbia.

The fishermen's mittens you see here are unlike any made today. The originals were knitted by Amantha Blake of South Brooksville, Maine, who knitted them by alternating two strands of creamy white yarn. They looked like every description I had heard of fishermen's mittens, but like none I had ever seen before: they were nearly a foot long — huge — and white. They were thick — a little puffy. Amantha Blake was a job knitter, who knit batches of mittens for shipment to a wholesaler in Boston who provided her yarn.

This type of knitting must have been commonly used for Maine fishermen's mittens at one time, or there would be no reason for a job knitter to use a method which takes more time to knit and consumes perhaps half again as much wool, unless this pair was different from the mittens she sold. All the Maine fishermen's mittens in use today, as well as those of Norway and Newfoundland, are simple single-knit white mittens, which thicken remarkably when

Robin Hansen

felted and shrunk, but none were as thick as these.

I saw my first pair of Amantha Blake mittens in Sweden! They had been given to Dalarnas Museum by their owner, Mary Anne Chase of South Brooksville, because the technique used to make them was similar to twined knitting, a technique discovered among the swedish peasantry and developed by Dalarnas Museum in the 1970s.

These were not, however, twined on the purl side: the two strands of yarn were alternated, with a yarn change after every stitch, giving the mittens the characteristically ridged appearance of bi-color knitting done by the right-hand method. Every seven or eight rounds, Blake had briefly changed the end she was carrying ahead, and alternated it for several rounds before knitting another eight rounds with the same strand ahead.

The mittens in Sweden and a similar pair in Chase's private collection in South Brookville may have been knit especially for family members or for local sale, and Blake may have developed the method herself from experience with bi-colored knitting. Unfortunately, we may never find out, as she died while Chase was in Sweden.

The first original fisherman's mitten I had access to was a pair knitted by Chebeague native Minnie Doughty, who died without teaching anyone how to knit fishermen's mittens. In her lifetime she had knitted many pairs and the pair that I examined was treasured as a keepsake by her daughters. These, too, may have been knitted with two strands, as they were extremely dense even though they had never been fulled.

Generally, fishermen's mittens are roughly the same. All are knitted of natural yarn, usually white, but sometimes gray. All are knitted very large and shrunk to size — until "they're molded to his hands," as Laura Ridgewell, the knitting wife of a Sebasco, Maine, fisherman told me. Everywhere they are knit large to be shrunk and fulled; and everywhere they are worn wet.

There are variations: Sometimes human hair was spun into the yarn or knitted in to improve durability and water resistance. In the Shetlands, gray fishermen's mittens are thought bit to be unlucky, which, knitting historian Sheila McGregor notes, makes sense because gray yarn does not shrink as well as white. In Norway, they are somtimes knitted with a thumb on each side to get maximum wear from both sides of the mitten.

Wear Wet Mittens Wet - but keep moving!

Albert Doughty of Bath, Maine, recounted going clamming with his father as an eight year old. He had brand new fishermen's mittens given him by his mother, and as he worked with his clam rake through the bed, and picked clams out with his fingers, he tried fastidiously to keep his mittens dry.

Finally, in exasperation his father said, "Looks like you're never gonna learn unless I show you." He took young Albert's mittens off, took them down to the water and "threw 'em in." After rescuing them, he wrung them out and gave them back. "Now put 'em on, and clap your hands like this," he said flinging his hands around his own shoulders to get the circulation moving. Albert never had cold hands again.

When I knew him he worked as an outdoor carpenter at the Bath Iron Works shipyard in Bath, Maine. Every winter morning he took his mittens to the edge of the river to wet them and wring them out. Often other carpenters with dry mittens had frostbitten fingers, but Albert never did.

Experimentation in our family shows that wet wool mittens are indeed warmer than dry ones, but only if you are working or playing hard. You are advised not to wet your mittens down before sitting on the front doorstep in a stiff, subzero wind.

Fishermen's Double-Knit Wet Mittens

Sizes: Child's 4-6 (Child's 8-10 years) Woman's Small (Woman's Medium) Man's Medium (Man's Large).

Needles: 1 set #4 dp knitting needles, or size you need to knit the correct gauge of 5.5 sts = 1 inch in pattern. This shrinks to 6.5 sts = 1 inch. 1 medium crochet hook. 1 yarn needle.

Materials: 4 ounces Bartlett Yarns 2-ply fisherman yarn or other fisherman wool yarn with lanolin. The mittens are traditionally cream-colored.

PATTERN

The cuff is traditionally knit in a k2, p1(or k3, p1) rib. This pattern uses k2, p1.

The rest of the mitten is knitted k1A, k1B, with A and B representing two strands of one color, usually sheep's white. The pattern is a simple one-one alteration of strands, which in two colors would be simplicity itself to keep straight. One strand is "carried ahead," the other drawn from behind. In Norwegian knitting this is called "stranding." If this doesn't make sense to you, pick up a piece of two-colored knitting and try this: k1 dark, k1 light, always taking the dark color from in front (or ahead, or from the left) of and from beneath the light strand. Always bring the light strand from behind (or the right) of the dark strand, and lift it over the dark strand before knitting it. If you knit with yarn in both hands, put the dark in the left, the light in the right. If you knit with the yarn on your left hand, place the dark strand farther down your index finger and the light strand closer to your index fingertip. The result is that the dark strand will stand up a little over the light strand in the fabric you are creating. In quick tight knitting, this emphasis is almost inevitable, and is often desirable. If you line the raised stitches up vertically, the whole fabric will be pulled in widthwise, and will be narrow, dense and very firm. If you

alternate the raised stitches, in a salt and pepper check, the fabric will tend to lie flat and wide and will be a little puffy — an ideal candidate for shrinking.

The difference between ordinary stranding and what you will be doing is that you're working in only one color. How can you be sure that two strands of the same color are being alternated in a one-one pattern offset by one stitch in each round? **First off**, you will always work on an uneven number of stitches, so you don't have to worry about the round before being offset by one stitch. It will be automatically. **Second**, identify one of the strands as the one to be carried ahead. What I do to keep the two strands sorted out is to thread a pony-tail elastic, or anything that lies loosely and inconspicuously around a finger, onto the second strand of yarn when it's joined at the top of the cuff. I put this over my right middle finger. This strand is always the one carried ahead. **Third**, if you get lost, or pick the knitting up after minutes or hours at something else, check and always use the strand that wasn't used for the last stitch.

If you make a mistake in one round, you will see every other stitch start to form a little vertical ridge in your knitting. Don't worry. The best and worst of this pattern is that it really doesn't show up at all after the mitten is shrunk and felted. But your gauge will be changed radically if there are more than one or two rounds of these vertical ridges together.

Winding yarn for knitting with two strands: The body of these mittens above the cuff are knitted with two strands of the same color yarn. You can use two balls, since the strands are not twisted together, but it's even more convenient to knit from both ends of the same ball of yarn. To do so, wind the yarn so that the end inside the

Fishermen's Mittens

ball is as accessible as the outside end. Wind the ball around a wooden spoon handle or use a crank winder, taking care to tie the starting end firmly around the stick first. When you're finished winding, slip the ball off the winder, then untie the inside end. You now have a two ended ball of yarn and can knit from both ends. Start from the inside end so you won't lose it, then join the outside end for the second strand at the top of the cuff.

NOW KNIT CUFF

On # 7 dp needles, cast on 33(36) 39(42) 45(51) on 3 needles. Divide these approximately evenly between 3 needles. If you have multiples of 3 on each needle, you can begin each needle with a knit stitch and so rib without thinking. K 2 p 1 with one strand until wristband measures 3(3) 3(4) 4(4) inches. Then join the second strand of yarn, thread a marker of some sort on it and hook the marker over one finger. Carry this strand ahead, and knit 1 st strand A, 1 st strand B from now on, never varying the pattern in the least except for increases and purl stitches. The pattern quickly falls into a fine rhythm and you can almost forget about it.

First round: Place last p st on first needle. P1, k1, knit 1 into the bar between two k sts, k1, p1. K rest of round, increasing a total of 6(7) 6(7) 6(6) stitches, evenly distributed, by knitting into the bar between 2 knit sts on the ribbing. Total = 41(43) 47(49) 53(59).

Second round: Start thumb gore: p1, inc 1 st in next st by knitting both strands into 1 st (in the correct order) k1, inc the same way in

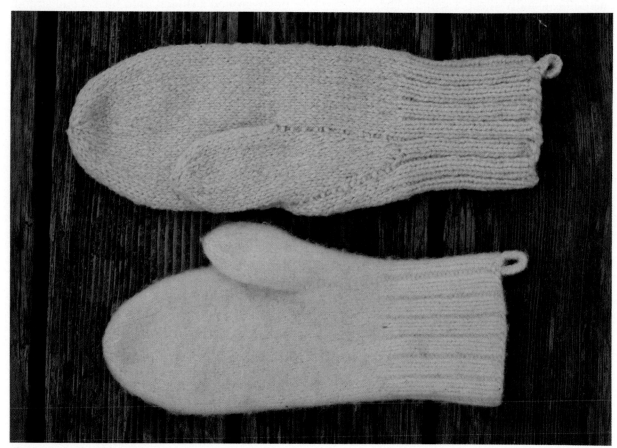

Fishermen's Mittens

the next st, p1. K around, and k rounds 3, 4, and 5, maintaining the same 2 p sts as markers.

Sixth round: P1, inc in next st k2, inc in next st, p1 (8 sts, including 2 p). K around. K3 more rounds. Continue to inc this way every fourth row until you have 11(13) 13(15) 17(19) sts for the thumb gore, including the 2 p sts. K 3 more rounds and place the thumb gore sts on a string including the p sts except in child's sizes 4-6 and 8-10. On these, leave the purl sts in the body of the mitten. Cast on 8 sts to bridge the gap and double- knit around. In the next round, k 2 together directly above the thumb hole once or twice to make a total 43(45) 49(53) 59(65) sts on 3 needles: K up 2(3) 3.25(3.75) 4(4.5) inches for the hand. You are ready to decrease for the tip of the fingers. This is complicated by the need to maintain pattern. Dec: K to 2 sts from end of needle, (SSK 2 together*. Next needle: K2 together, then knit to 2 sts from end of needle) and repeat around. The last k2 together decrease will be on the first two sts of the first needle in the next round.

*SSK 2 together: Named and developed by Elizabeth Zimmerman, this old technique makes a neat decrease that leans left. Use for the first of two decreases that lie side by side. Slip 1 st as if to k, slip next st as if to k, slip both sts back onto left needle by placing left needle into right (not left) side of both stitches, k these 2 sts together.
Repeat this dec round every third round until there are 19 sts left. K2 together around. Ten stitches remain. K1 round, break yarn with about a six-inch tail. Thread this onto a yarn needle, and firmly draw up the remaining sts on the trail. Darn the end back and forth through the tip of the mitten, concealing the sts in the knit.

THUMB
Pick up from thumb gore 9(11) 13(15) 17(19) sts divided between 2 needles and pick up and twist 1 st from each side of thumb hole. On the two child's sizes, pick up the 2 purl sts without twisting them. Pick up the 8 sts from the hand side on the third needle. Total sts: 19(21) 23(25) 27(29). K 2 rounds. Next round, dec 1 st on both ends of the third needle, and redistribute the sts so there are about the same number on each. K straight up until the thumb measures 1.8(2.4) 2.4(2.75) 2.75(3) inches. Next round, dec k2 together, k2, and repeat around. K1 round. Next round: k2 together, k1, and repeat around. Pull end through the remaining sts and darn through tip of thumb, concealing sts in the knit. Crochet a loop at edge of cuff for hanging the mittens to dry. Use the tail left from casting on if possible. Minnie Doughty also buttonhole-stitched the loop for extra strength. Work any remaining ends into the back of the fabric. This is a good time to check and cover up holes at the corner of the thumb hole.

SHRINKING
Traditionally fishermen's mittens are felted, or fulled, by the fisherman on his boat. To do this, he wets his mittens in the hot cooling water from the engine, tosses them on the cold, wet, salty deck and walks on them while he works, sloshing cold water on them in the process. After a while, he dries them on the engine manifold, carefully turning them so they don't singe. Then he wets them in cold water, or hot, and starts the process over again. It takes a day or two to shrink them to size doing this.

Here is a shortcut for fishermen who don't care to do the above or for non-fishermen.

Fishermen's Mittens

What shrinks the mitten is not the hot water or the cold water, but the shock of going from one to the other. Fulling instructions I found in Vibeke Lind's *Knit in the Nordic Tradition* suggest a controlled method to get the same results. To simulate the changes in temperature a fisherman's mitten faces, use hot soapy water and cold rinse water. The soap makes the little hooked wool fibers slip past one another more easily. Lind says: *the hotter the hot water and the colder the cold water, the more shrinkage there will be. The more soap there is in the hot water, the faster the shrinkage and felting will be. The more one rubs and kneads the wool the more the knitted fabric will mat together into a continuous, weather-impervious fabric. Add to this: Fishermen in Maine and Nova Scotia hold that cold salt water shrinks more than cold fresh water.*

So get together the following materials, and let's shrink:
a pair of too-big wool mittens; a washboard or bumpy surface to rub on (a pastry-cooling rack laid across the corner of the kitchen sink works well); lots of boiling water; lots of icy cold water (add ice if you want); sea salt; Murphy's Oil Soap, Johnson's Baby Shampoo, or other real soap; and two plastic dishpans or other containers that size.

First for your own satisfaction, trace around one mitten on a sheet of newspaper. Then you'll know not only if it shrinks but also how much it shrinks where. You may want to knit your next pair longer or narrower. Stir soap into one bowl with water as hot as your hands can stand and fill the other bowl with icy cold rinse water as cold as your hands can stand. Dissolve salt in the cold water if you want to, about a tablespoon per gallon. Submerge the mittens in the hot soapy water and squeeze water through them. Let them set to get used to the heat. (What a shock they're going to get!) Then scrub them on a bumpy surface, repeatedly wetting them in the hot soapy water until they begin to look fuzzy or until you feel like moving on to something else. Then squeeze them out and plunge them into the cold water and rinse all the soap out. You'll actually feel the wool tense up as you do this. Change the water to keep it cold and clear. Squeeze, but don't wring, the cold water out. Then back to the hot water with them and more soap and scrubbing and rubbing. Replenish the hot water as needed and add soap each time. Rub some soap right into the mitten.

Repeat this back and forth from hot to cold four or five times. I sometimes let them rest after a cold salt rinse, squeezed out on the drainboard, thinking their torment is over, while I have breakfast or a cup of coffee. Then back into more hot soapy water with them and more scrubbing. After a few such violent changes, you'll feel a change in the texture of the fabric. It will feel thicker, stiffer and tighter, and will be visibly smaller in the cold water. If you've knitted in natural white wool, it will also be much whiter than when you started. Put a table-spoon or two of vinegar in a last cold water rinse to soften the wool, squeeze the rinse thoroughly through the mittens, then squeeze them out for good. Roll them up in a towel and lean on them to remove excess water. Now the finishing touch that fisher-men don't do but you can: take a stiff brush, like a vegetable brush (I squeeze the straws of a whisk broom together at the bottom) and brush the mitten from cuff toward the fingertips. Brush and brush, and all the fuzzed fibers that aren't matted will go one way and look beautiful. The whole shrink-ing and brushing procedure for one pair of mittens may take up to 90 minutes. When dried, your mittens will look like Maine fishermen's mittens knitted by a little old lady in Sweden for her favorite grandson.

Dot Ratigan

When I interviewed Dot, we began our conversation with a discussion of how often people fail to recognize that knitting is an art form and a substantial career for many men and women. A morning spent with Dot and a look at her extensive portfolio, leaves no doubt that this is a serious line of work for her, as it is for many of the other people I have met through this business. To call Dot the premier designer of knitting patterns in Maine would not be an overstatement and she certainly must have as many years in the business as anyone.

Growing up in New York City, surrounded by an extended family of first generation Irish immigrants, Dot was inspired by many creative women. From them, she learned a variety of skills including tatting, sewing, needlepoint, embroidery, and knitting. Dot observed much from watching one of her aunts who was a talented dressmaker. Sewing skills learned from her are now a reference point when Dot tackles a difficult project.

Dot was trained as a registered nurse, a profession she worked at for over 20 years, much of that time in Saranac Lake, NY. One day, while walking through the village, Dot was considering a more creative career. The local yarn shop came into view and she thought to herself, "There's a profession I'd like to know more about." She talked the owner into selling her the business and then ran it for nearly ten years, the last three of which were in Maine.

Owning a yarn shop rounded out Dot's years of knitting experience, preparing her for a career in design. She became familiar with almost every yarn on the market and how they performed. She taught classes in all different crafts — crewel, needlepoint, knitting — whatever people wanted to learn. She also assisted those customers who looked at patterns and said, "I like this sweater, but..." Dot would then take over, designing sweaters to suit their needs. After becoming proficient while serving her customers, Dot realized her design, instruction, and writing skills had commercial value.

She sold her first design to the Bernat Yarn Company. A salesman had come by and given her some yarn from a new line. Dot was so pleased to receive the yarn that she used it to construct a hat for him. He loved the hat and showed it off at his next sales meeting. Bernat bought the pattern from Dot and it ended up being a classic, staying on the market for the next fifteen years until the Bernat company closed.

Dot has attended The National Needlework Association's New York trade show every year since its beginnings in 1975, and it was on one of these visits that she took the step that propelled her into the world of knitting designers. Before leaving for the show, she went to her local supermarket and bought every magazine that featured a knitting pattern and then called and asked for appointments with the magazine's knitting editors. When Dot arrived in New York, she was armed with 19 different creations, including the sweater her son, Steve, was wearing as he drove her to the airport. It was a cold January day and when

Dot Ratigan

Dot decided she needed it at the last minute he willingly agreed to drive home in his T-shirt. After she had met with all of the editors, selling them all something different, she returned home with only two items left.

That long day in New York led to a prolific career in the field of knitting. Dot has designed sweaters for virtually every major women's and craft magazine and most of the yarn companies. She is well known as a designer of quality Aran sweaters and she was one of six designers who had their work featured in the 1989 book, *Vogue Knitting*. Dot doesn't limit herself to Aran sweaters, however. She can work in such varied styles as Norwegian, Fair Isle, lacework, intarsia, and textured designs, and she enjoys working with all kinds of fibers.

Yarn companies or magazine editors are well known for their habit of calling designers on a Friday and insisting that they need a certain design by the following Tuesday. It is on jobs such as these that Dot's years of experience come in handy. She has worked with virtually every fiber and can translate an idea from her head, through her hands, into a design. She conceives a sweater in her head, draws a rough sketch, and sits down and knits it. Dot knits every sweater she designs, carefully working out any bugs in the pattern, then translates the pattern to her Macintosh computer, producing both graphs and written patterns.

Today, Dot does far more than designing. She is consulting editor for two magazines, and the knitting editor for *Knitters* magazine. As the owner of Pine Tree Knitters, she is also a business woman. Her company produces ski hats, scarves, sweaters, and headbands for retail outlets including L. L. Bean. Dot is the head designer, production manager, sales agent, invoicer, packer, and shipper. She employs local people who produce the designs on knitting machines and hand finish them. The business produces approximately 5000 hand finished pieces each year.

I could go on at length describing Dot's versatility and accomplishments, but perhaps far more important is her philosophy toward knitting and her commitment to knitting as an art. Dot is a dedicated teacher. She is an instructor for the National Needlework Association and leads a regular, monthly knitting group. She reads and studies knitting, discusses ideas with other designers, and is convinced that you "should share your knowledge." She strongly believes that knitting is an "art that should be handed down to others." As long as there are knitters with Dot's tremendous skill willing to generously pass on what they know, I am confident that knitting will continue to be recognized as an art and craft.

Big 'n Little Diamonds

Big 'n Little Diamonds

Size: 8 (10, 12, 14) To fit chest 27 (28, 30, 32)" Overall length 17 (18¼, 19, 20¼)" Sleeve length 11 (12, 13½, 15)"

Materials: Brown Sheep's Nature Spun sportweight Color #250 Petal 3 100 gm skeins

Needles: Size 4 & 7. Size 5 16" circular needle. Cable needle (cn) Holders

Gauge: 6 sts and 8 rows = 1" worked over stockinette st

PATTERNS USED

Pattern 1: Twisted cable rib, Row 1: (WS) *k1, p2, rep from *, end k1. Row 2: *p1, k2tog, then k the first st again, rep from *, end p1.

Pattern 2: Moss stitch, Row 1: *k1, p1, rep from *. Rows 2 & 4: k the knits and p the purls. Row 3: *p1, k1, rep from *.

Pattern 3: Right plaited cable, Row 1: p2 (2, 2, 3), k3, place 3 sts on cn to back, k3, k3 on cn, p2 (2, 2, 3). Rows 2 & 4: k2 (2, 2, 3), p9, k2 (2, 2, 3). Row 3: p2 (2, 2, 3), place 3 sts on cn to front, k3, k3 on cn, k3, p2 (2, 2, 3).

Pattern 4: Left plaited cable

Row 1: p2 (2, 2, 3), place 3 sts on cn to front, k3, k3 on cn, k3, p2 (2, 2, 3).

Rows 2 & 4: k2 (2, 2, 3), p9, k2 (2, 2, 3).

Row 3: p2 (2, 2, 3), k3, place 3 sts on cn to back, k3, k3 on cn, p2 (2, 2, 3).

Pattern 5: Shell rib, Row 1: tw2 (Twist 2- k2tog, then k the first st again), p2, (k1, yo) 4 times, k1, p2, tw2. Row 2: p2, k2, (p1, k1) 4 times, p1, k2, p2. Row 3: tw2, p2, k1, p1, ssk, k1, k2tog, p1, k1, p2, tw2. Row 4: p2, k2, p1, k1, p3tog, k1, p1, k2, p2.

Pattern 6: Big 'n little diamonds, Row 1: p7, place next 3 sts on cn to front, k2b, place one st back on left hand needle and p, k2b on cn, p7. Row 2 and all even rows: k the knits and p the purls. Row 3: p6, PRC (purl right cross-place next st on cn to back, k2b, p1 on cn), k1, PLC (purl left cross-place next 2 sts on cn to front, p1, k2b on cn), p6. Row 5: p5, PRC, k1, p1, k1, PLC, p5. Row 7: p4, PRC, (k1, p1) 2 times, k1, PLC, p4. Row 9: p3, PRC, (k1, p1) 3 times, k1, PLC, p3. Row 11: p2, PRC, (k1, p1) 4 times, k1, PLC, p2. Row 13: p2, PLC, (p1, k1) 4 times, p1, PRC, p2. Row 15: p3, PLC, (p1, k1) 3 times, p1, PRC, p3. Row 17: p4, PLC, (p1, k1) 2 times, p1, PRC, p4. Row 19: p5, PLC, p1, k1, p1, PRC, p5. Row 21: p6, PLC, p1, PRC, p6. Row 23: rep Row 1. Row 25: rep Row 3. Row 27: rep Row 5. Row 29: rep Row 7. Row 31: rep Row 17. Row 33: rep Row 19. Row 35: rep Row 21.

BACK

With smaller needle, cast on 91 (97, 103, 109) sts. Work 2 rows of Pattern 1 for $1^3/4$ (2, 2, $2^1/4$)" ending on row 2. Set-up row: WS facing, p 6 (7, 9, 10), inc 1, p 6 (8, 9, 9), inc 1 (0, 0, 0), k2 (2, 2, 3), p9, k2 (2, 2, 3), p2, k1, inc 1, p5, inc 1, k1, p2, k7, p2, k1, p2, k7, p2, k1, inc 1, p5, inc 1, k1, p2, k2 (2, 2, 3), p9, k2 (2, 2, 3), inc 1 (0, 0, 0), p 6 (8, 9, 9), inc 1, p 6 (7, 9, 10). 99 (103, 109, 115) sts. Change to larger needles. Work Row 1 of: Pattern 2 over 14 (16, 19, 20) sts, Pattern 3 over 13 (13, 13, 15) sts, Pattern 5 over 13 sts, Pattern 6 over 19 sts, Pattern 5 over 13 sts, Pattern 4 over 13 (13, 13, 15) sts, Pattern 2 over 14 (16, 19, 20) sts. Work in patterns as established until 10 ($10^1/2$, 11, $11^3/4$)" from beginning. Mark each end of needle for sleeve placement. Work even until 7 ($7^3/4$, 8, $8^1/2$)" above underarm markers. Place sts on spare holder.

FRONT

Work as for back until $14^3/4$(16, $16^3/4$, 18)" from beginning ending ready to work row 4 of pattern 5. Work 40 (42, 43, 47) sts, place center 19 (19, 23, 23) sts on holder, join yarn, work to end of row. Working both sides at same time, dec 2 sts each neck edge every other row 2 times, then dec 1 st each neck edge every 4 rows 3 times. Work until same length as back. Knit and bind off 33 (35, 36, 40) shoulder sts on front and back together. With circular needle, pick up 81 (81, 93, 93) sts around neck including sts on holders and work in Pattern 1 for 1", p1 row, work in stockinette st for 1". Sew live sts to inside of neck edge.

SLEEVES

(WS) with larger needle, pick up 100 (110, 114, 122) sts between underarm markers. Row 1: work 35 (40, 38, 42) sts in Pattern 2, (p2, tw2) 7 (7, 9, 9) times, p2, work 35 (40, 38, 42) sts in Pattern 2. Continue in established patterns dec 1 st each end of needle every 4 rows 18 (20, 21, 24) times. Work until 9 (10, $11^1/2$, 13)" from shoulder or desired length. Dec all p2 patterns to p1 and dec last row to 52 (52, 58, 58) sts. Change to smaller needles and work in Pattern 1 for 2". Bind off. Finishing: Sew side and sleeve seams. Optional: Embroider flowers in diamonds.

Carol Loehr

Carol Loehr is a designer and creator of the very element that drives the other women in this book — yarn. Carol supervises every detail, beginning with her flock's genetic make up, through lambing, shearing, and all of the way to choosing the mix of the fleeces. In doing so, she creates a wonderful product.

The yarn is sold through Carol's business, Swans Island Farm, named after the island where she has been a resident for fourteen years. On the day I visited, her flock numbered 32 ewes, 28 lambs, and 3 rams, with 12 more ewes yet to deliver. Carol is constantly experimenting with cross breeding, looking for the right sheep to suit her particular island situation. She started her flock with Border Cheviots, a breed known for its hardiness and high quality fleece. Over the years she has mixed in North Country Cheviots, a larger sheep of the same breed. Border Cheviots are slightly less domesticated, compared with the North Country sheep. This is an important consideration for an island flock whose members often forage in rugged, half-overgrown pastures and live through the winter in minimal shelters.

Carol's most recent introduction to the flock is her registered Shetland ram. The Shetland is a very small sheep, slightly larger than a medium sized dog, that is a little easier for her to handle physically, an important consideration for a woman who works primarily alone. The Shetland comes in all colors and the rams have horns. Once the dominant breed on the Shetland Islands, many flocks were let go during the Second World War as shepherds went off to join the army. After the war, when sheep breeders' interests turned toward larger, meatier breeds, Shetlands were interbred and the numbers of purebred sheep dwindled sufficiently for them to be considered endangered.

Their numbers are now growing again, although it is still very expensive to purchase one of these fine wooled sheep. Carol has bred her Shetland ram with the Cheviot ewes hoping to create a sheep uniquely suited to her circumstances and possessing the wool knitters have sought out for centuries. She is planning to purchase a Shetland ewe this fall and start a purebred Shetland flock which will add more subtle colors and fineness to the wool.

Carol owns only two and one-half acres but makes use of up to 100 acres on the island for hay and pasture, "borrowing" the land from both year-round and summer residents. We walked down through the fields across the road from her house, and ended up on a seaside pasture. Carol had fenced the pasture off with temporary plastic fencing which she can move as the sheep clear an area. These sheep have a wonderful view, looking out to other islands and the occasional fishing and sailboats that pass by. These sheep come "home" every night to a moveable barn built by Carol. With wood frame feeders forming the walls and reinforced plastic roof, the structure can be dismantled by Carol at the end of every season and moved to another area of the newly cleared field, enriching the soil with the remains of the "barn" floor.

Later we drove to a neighbor's barn that was home to another part of Carol's flock. Carol needed to check on an lamb with an ailing foot — a never ending part of the shepherd's chores. This location is also home to "Big Fella," a handsome Holstein ox which is part of Carol's extended menagerie.

There is a third barn just below her house where Carol sorts her fleeces. A specially built rack allows Carol to pick over the fleeces and remove any parts she doesn't want spun into the yarn. After all of the individual fleeces are "skirted" (picked over), she hand spins samples of the different fleeces together to determine what combination yields a yarn she is happy with. She then tags and marks each fleece and tells the mill what percentage of each fleece to use to duplicate the samples. To produce colored yarns, she must also instruct the mill how much of the colored wools to mix with the white for each shade she desires.

Once the wool is returned to Carol, one step remains before shipping it to her eager customers. Since the returned product resembles string more than yarn, she must wash it to give it softness. This is done by tying the skeins in four places and setting them in the washing machine with hot water and a mild detergent. After soaking for about 15 minutes, the yarn is run through the washer's gentle spin cycle and the resulting product is soft, fluffy, and strong. The yarn is then hung on large cardboard tubes and lightly weighted to keep it uniform as it dries.

Sheep are the focus of Carol's farm, but they certainly are not the only thing in her very eclectic life. When the gate is opened to her diverse, small farm, one is struck by an abundance of living things. A rooster crows, chickens peck at new shoots, rabbits of varying colors amble contentedly across the lawn. One's eyes focus on Carol's octagonal shaped house, which she designed and built and has plans to expand someday. Inside there is evidence of Carol's many talents — the upholstery project she is working on, the Locker hooked rugs she creates from combed and carded fleece, and the details of her house interior she has put together with many reclaimed materials and treasures gathered on her travels.

Carol's mostly full time job is restoring old houses, a business she runs with two full time partners. They replace and restore old plaster and woodwork, paint and hang wallpaper, and have in the past rebuilt the foundations and restored the exteriors of old island

Photo by Jeff Dworsky

houses. As Carol put it, "This business of making a living interferes with a lot," and clearly Carol has many irons in the fire. Along with her animals and Carol's many crafts, she is also busy selling her latest product, "Sea Soil." The day I was visiting, Islanders were stopping by with baskets and barrels to buy this soil amendment created by composting fish wastes with peat moss mined from a mainland bog. This spring's product is the first produced and Carol has hopes that the business will continue to expand.

If Carol's life now is a diverse collection of varied activities, her past has been no different. Trained in apparel design at Rhode Island School of Design, Carol has had dissimilar careers — she has been a model, an airline stewardess, bathing suit designer, and she has spent time "messing about in boats." In Carol's words, "Life in rural Maine, particularly on an island, requires a diversity of occupations that often change with the season. I'm not the person that wants to do the same thing forever and ever." It doesn't look like there is any danger of this in Carol's present or future.

Nan Hadden

Nan Hadden created Woolies Hand-knits, a ten-year-old business that is very successful. With Nan serving as sole designer and company president, the business produces almost 3000 handknit sweaters a year, all knit in Uruguay. A spring and fall line are created every year, each composed of 14 to 20 designs.

Nan got her start as a designer when she was just a child. Her first formal lesson came when she was seven, under the watchful eye of a German nun who taught classes at a local convent in Pittsburgh, where Nan grew up. She learned to knit using the continental method, producing the standard first project — a scarf. Throughout her childhood she continued to be interested in knitting and other handcrafts and took drawing lessons from a neighbor who was a professional artist. Her strongest knitting inspiration was a neighbor who could knit Norwegian sweaters without a pattern, and was even able to sit and talk while she worked out complicated designs.

In her teens, Nan determined that her mother was more likely to pay for fabric and a pattern than a clothes-shopping trip to the mall. After spending a lot of time sewing, Nan decided she wanted to be a fashion designer. She studied Fine Arts in college and went on to pursue a variety of jobs, along with getting married and having a son and daughter.

In 1980 Nan started experimenting with traditional Norwegian sweaters, reshaping them to give an updated twist to a classic look. She liked what she was creating and decided to find a few knitters to make samples for her. She took these sweaters to stores in New York and Boston, where she was living, and secured about $2000 in orders. When the stores began calling her back and asking what she was going to do next, she knew she had a business.

At this point, Nan had no business experience, no money to invest, and no conventional design skills. In spite of this, She decided to proceed, trusting that if she just went slowly enough and didn't get in over her head, she could probably make it work. At first she kept her job, coordinating the knitting on the side, but after two years, she plunged into the business full time.

From the beginning, the demand for her sweaters was always greater than production, and her business doubled every year. Nan was aware of the many British designers selling handknits in this country and was interested in capturing some of those same markets with her domestically produced sweaters. Aware that the British sweaters were produced in rural areas where there was a longstanding tradition of good knitters, she speculated that a similar tradition existed in New England. She began working with rural home knitters from Maine, Vermont, and New Hampshire, and at one point as many as 100 women were knitting her sweaters, greatly increasing her production.

In 1984, a controversy raging in Congress over the legality of producing knitwear at home changed Nan's business. Nan was visited by Department of Labor inspectors who investigated her home-knitting enterprise. They determined that her knitters were not contract laborers, as she had assumed, and that she should have been treating them as employees, paying hourly wages, social security, and other routine costs. She was given a choice — pay $80,000 in fees and back payments or cease knitting immediately and put these women out of work. Lacking both the money and stamina required to fight the federal bureaucracy, Nan decided to give up on domestic production. She contacted her knitters, explained the situation, and advised them that the sweater they were currently working on would be the last one for her. Her knitters were furious and many of them contacted their congress people to express their views. Nan felt it was ironic that when she asked the Labor Department how they suggested she continue in business, they recommended that she "go out of the country and use foreign knitters — like everyone else." To her it seemed like a strange way to protect our labor force.

Nan was determined to keep her business going and initially worked with knitters

in Great Britain before settling in 1987 on an arrangement with knitters in Uruguay. Sales of sweaters with the updated Norwegian look were still healthy, but Nan was concerned that interest in those designs would soon start to fade. More importantly, as a designer she was ready to try something else.

She then began exploring a look that is now her trademark, known in the ready-to-wear business as "fancy sweaters." Nan combines colors and patterns using intarsia knitting, classic embroidery, and textured knitting to create "surface interest." Historic textiles are often her source of inspiration and she consults many books for representations of design from the 16th century on. She looks at such things as needlepoint,

Nan Hadden

rugs, crewel, and fabric, and has made trips to museums in England to look for inspiration. Over the past two years, Nan has been concentrating on the development of this look of her own and her business continues to grow.

The design process often begins for Nan when she sees something like an old piece of embroidery and considers how it might translate into knitwear. She then begins imagining what shape of garment would complement this motif and considers how to work the fabric pattern into the design — whether it will repeat itself, be represented as mirror images, or become part of a random pattern.

She next draws a rough sketch showing the general shape and details, and then determines the specs for the garment — width, length, shape of the neckline. Most of the shapes that Nan works with are not too fussy, rather oversized garments with a minimum of fitting. She often adds variety in the ribbing and collars.

The last step in Nan's designing process is to work out the pattern, freehand, on graph paper. She begins by mapping the outlines and shaping the sweater as she figures it all out mathematically and then plugs in the design elements. After graphing, she reduces her drawing with a copier and begins experimenting with her colored pencils to determine the colors.

Once all of the decisions are made, she assigns each color a letter and symbol and starts the final graphs, which can be very complicated for some of her more ornate designs. Because all of the sweaters, including the samples, will be knit in Uruguay, she sends detailed instructions even though she has never knit the actual garment. Along with the graph, she provides a more formal sketch to show the knitters what the finished sweater should look like. She provides drawings of all components with specs and notes on every stitch to be used. All of this information is conveyed to Uruguay via FAX machine or the mail with occasional questions discussed over the phone.

Designing is very "cerebral" for Nan — everything is visualized and thought out in her mind before being translated to a piece of paper. It is something she does alone in her studio, and her concentration is often so intense that hours may pass by without her noticing. She hates to have the distraction of the phone ringing — something that is often unavoidable when you are the owner of the business as well as the designer.

One task that Nan doesn't have to assume is that of marketing her goods. Her work is sold through a sales representative with a showroom in New York. The rep handles all of the orders for Nan's products, and over the years has sold to such stores as Paul Stuart, Nordstrom, Lord & Taylor, Brooks Brothers, and now several stores in Japan.

The business sells over $300,000 worth of sweaters a year, with all the work handled by Nan, her team of knitters, the sales rep and a part-time bookkeeper. Nan finds great satisfaction in her work and has learned over the years that although she must handle both design and business matters, working as a designer is clearly her niche. She is happy to see her style evolving and now says, "I like what I am doing, and the public is buying." What more could a designer ask for?

Odessa

Finished Size: 36(40,44)"
Finished Length: 23"
Needles: Size 5 and 7 or size needed to
   obtain stitch gauge of 5 sts and 7 rows =
   1" using larger needles over stockinette
   stitch
   One pair each size needle 4, 5 & 6
   One 16" circular needle
   Bobbins
   Stitch holders
Materials: Sweater is knitted in worsted
   weight wool.
   5 4-oz skeins black (MC)
   250 yds olive; 100 yards curry
   150 yds cranberry; 85 yds mulberry
   75 yds mulberry tweed
   50 yds powder blue; 30 yds cobalt
   30 yds cornflower

NOTES
Please read all instructions before beginning this sweater.
1. The entire design is based on the above gauge. It is important to do a stitch and row gauge before beginning. The outer margins are marked with a dotted circle in twelve areas. If you are unable to obtain the same row gauge (even after changing needle sizes), or need to lengthen or shorten the sweater, then add or delete a row in Main Color (MC) on these marked rows in order to obtain the desired length.
2. An edge stitch in the MC for each size is marked on the graph with a long rectangular box.
3. The center stitch on the body and sleeve graphs is marked with a double heavy line as a reference point.
4. Read graphs from right to left on right side rows and from left to right on wrong side rows.

5. Knit body and sleeves in stockinette stitch using Fair Isle, intarsia and duplicate stitch technique.
6. To begin, wind bobbins of Contrasting Colors (CC) except Cobalt and Cornflower.
7. For best results, work the flowers (Cobalt and Cornflower) in the small vine pattern in between the larger patterns in duplicate stitch.
8. Use separate bobbins of the same color on either side of the center of the larger designs in order to eliminate long floats in the pattern.
9. When changing colors, bring new yarn from beneath yarn just used to avoid holes.
10. Work in pattern following graph to underarm markers (see Margin Key) and then follow instructions for given size.

BACK
Using larger needles and MC, cast on 82 (90, 98) sts. Change to smaller needles and work as follows:
Row 1. (RS) K2, *P2, K2, rep from *.
Row 2. P2, *K2, P2, rep from *. Rep these 2 rows for 3", inc 11 (13, 15) sts evenly spaced over last row of ribbing — 93 (103, 113) sts. Change to larger needles and follow graph to underarm markers. **Shape armhole:** Bind off 7 sts at the beg of the next 2 rows. Dec 1 st on the inside of edge st every 4th row 4 times — 71(81, 91) sts. Continue following graph to Back neck marker. **Shape neck:** Work in pattern across 23 (26, 30) sts, place next 25 (29, 31) sts on holder for Back neck, join new ball of MC and work in pattern to end of row. Dec 1 st at each neck edge every other row 5 times. Work to end of graph. Work 1 row in MC. Place remaining 18 (21, 25) sts on holder for each shoulder.

Odessa

FRONT

Work as for Back to Front neck marker.
Shape neck: Work in pattern across 27 (30, 34) sts, place next 17 (21, 23) sts on holder for Front neck, join new ball of MC and work in pattern to end of row. Working both sides at the same time, dec 1 st at each neck edge every other row 9 times. Work to end of graph. Work 1 row in MC. Place remaining 18 (21, 25) sts on holder for each shoulder.

SLEEVES

Using larger needles and MC, cast on 46 sts. Change to smaller needles and work ribbing as for Back for 2¹/₂", inc 11 sts evenly spaced over last row of ribbing — 57 sts. Change to larger needles and maintaining 1

edge st, follow graph to end working incs as shown on graph. Bind off sts loosely.

FINISHING

Place shoulder sts on needles and with right sides facing, knit shoulders together. Sew in sleeves to armhole openings. Sew side and sleeve seams. With MC and largest circular needle, starting at left shoulder neck seam, pick up 15 sts down left front, 17 (21, 23) sts on Front holder, 15 sts up right front, 8 sts down right back, 25 (29, 31) sts on Back holder, 8 sts up left back — 88 (96, 100) sts. Work in K2, P2 rib for 1". Change to medium size circular needle and work in rib for 1". Change to smallest size circular needle and work in rib for 1". Bind off loosely with largest needle. Weave in all ends.

Sleeve Chart

COLOR KEY

MARGIN KEY

	Main Color (MC)		■ Mulberry Tweed	* Add or subtract rows for proper length
	Curry		■ Cranberry	□ Edge stitch
	Olive		• Mulberry	
	Cornflower		◤ Rose	
	Cobalt		○ Powder Blue	

Front & Back Chart

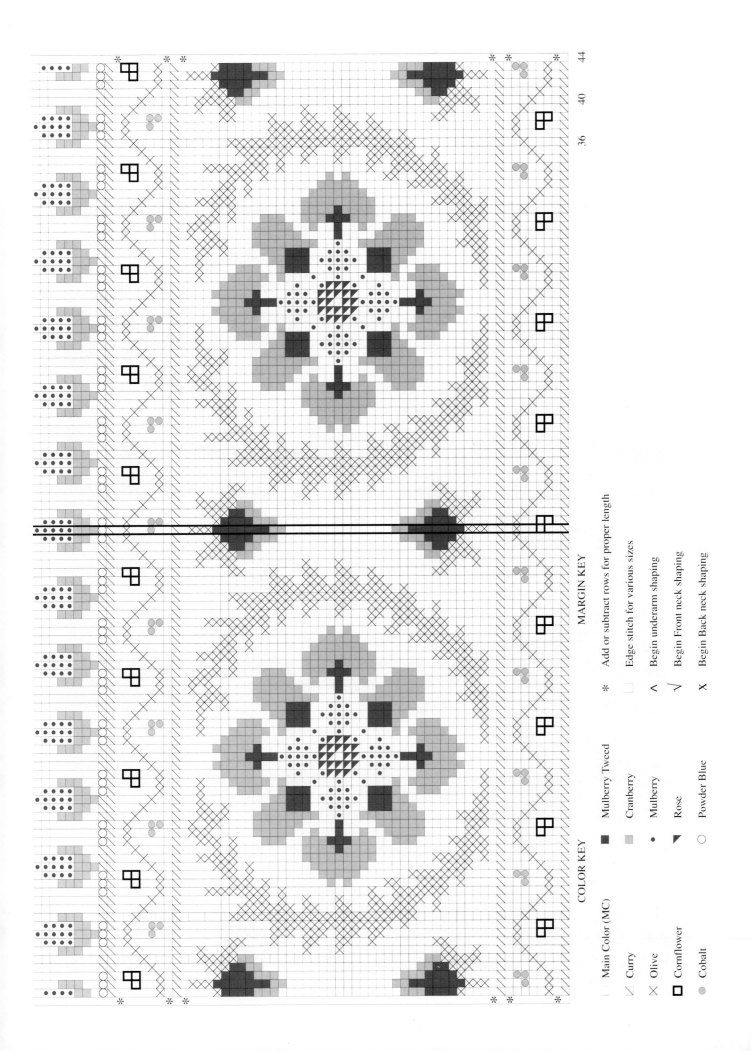

44

40

36

MARGIN KEY

*   Add or subtract rows for proper length

▢   Edge stitch for various sizes

∧   Begin underarm shaping

√   Begin Front neck shaping

✕   Begin Back neck shaping

COLOR KEY

☐ Main Color (MC)   ■ Mulberry Tweed

╱ Curry   ▨ Cranberry

✕ Olive   • Mulberry

▢ Cornflower   ◤ Rose

● Cobalt   ○ Powder Blue

Odessa

Samarkand

Samarkand

Sizes: 38(40,42)
Finished Size: 40(42,44)"
Finished length: 26"
Needles: Size 4 and 6 or size needed to
    obtain stitch gauge of 6 sts and 8 rows =
    1" using larger needles over
    stockinette stitch
    Size 5 16" circular needle
    Bobbins
    Stitch holders
    Tapestry needle
Materials: Sweater is knitted in worsted
    weight yarns.
    1200 yds red (MC), 360 yds lilac
    240 yds canvas, 125 yds olive
    120 yds blue, 100 yds curry

NOTES
Please read all instructions before beginning this sweater.
1. The entire design is based on the above gauge. It is important to do a stitch and row gauge before beginning. Make any adjustment in body length before beginning border pattern. Sleeves may be adjusted after working sleeve pattern.
2. An edge stitch in the MC for each size is marked on the graph with a long rectangular box.
3. The center stitch on the body and sleeve graphs is marked with a double heavy line as a reference point.
4. Read graphs from right to left on right side rows and from left to right on wrong side rows.
5. All ribs are k1, p1 in color B. Knit the body and sleeves in stockinette stitch.
6. The ground color of individual sections is either "A" or "B". This is shown on the chart by the letters written in the individual sections. There is only partial patterning on the Back and Sleeves. The ground color for the Back and Sleeves is A.

7. Wind bobbins with different colors. Use separate bobbins of the same color on either side of the center of the larger designs in order to eliminate long floats in the pattern.
8. When changing colors, bring new yarn from beneath yarn just used to avoid holes.
9. Work sleeves from graph increasing as indicated.

BACK
Using smaller needles and B, cast on 123 (129, 135) sts. *Row 1:* K1, *p1, k1, repeat from *. *Row 2:* P1, *k1, p1, repeat from *. Repeat these 2 rows for 1". Change to larger needles and work Border pattern using Midnight Blue for ground color. Work body graph (*see note 7*) to armhole. **Shape armhole:** Bind off 5 (8, 11) sts at beg of next 2 rows. Dec 2 sts at each end of every other row 5 times — 93 sts (all sizes). Continue following graph to Back neck shaping.
Shape neck: Work in pattern across 34 sts, place next 25 sts on holder for Back neck, join new ball of MC and work in pattern to end of row. Working both sides at the same time, bind off 2 sts at each neck edge 5 times. Dec 1 st at each neck edge *every* row 5 times, then every other row once. Work to end of graph. Place remaining 18 sts on holder for each shoulder.

FRONT
Work as for Back to Front neck shaping.
Shape neck: Work in pattern across 36 sts, place next 21 sts on holder for Front neck, join new ball of MC and work in pattern to end of row. Working both sides at the same time, bind off 2 sts at each neck edge 3 times. Dec 1 st at each neck edge *every* row 7 times, then every other row 5 times. Work to end of graph. Place remaining 18 sts on holder for each shoulder.

SLEEVES:

Using smaller needles and B, cast on 55 sts. Work ribbing as for Back. Change to larger needles and work Border pattern using Midnight Blue for ground color. Maintaining 1 edge st, follow graph inc 1 st every sixth row till 89 sts remain. Then inc 1 st every fourth row till 109 sts remain then continue straight to desired length. Bind off sts loosely.

FINISHING:

Place shoulder sts on needles and with right sides facing, knit shoulders sts together. Using circular needle and B, pick up 114(120,126) sts around neck edge. *K1, p1, repeat from * for 1". Bind off loosely with larger needle. Sew in sleeves to armhole openings. Sew side and sleeve seams. Weave in all ends.

Sleeve Chart

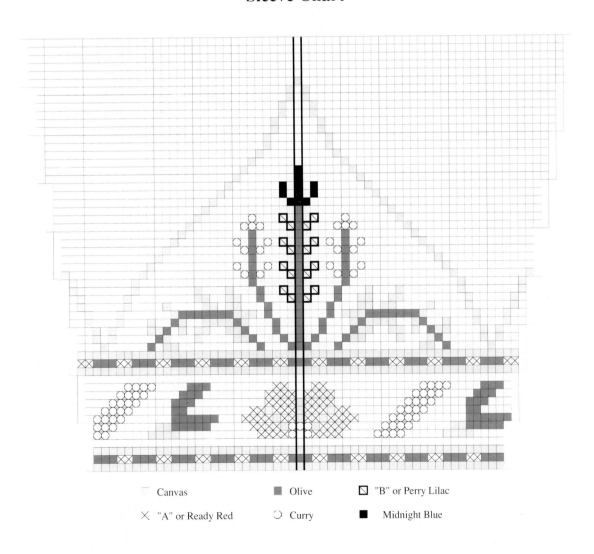

⁻ Canvas	■ Olive	◨ "B" or Perry Lilac
✕ "A" or Ready Red	○ Curry	■ Midnight Blue

Samarkand

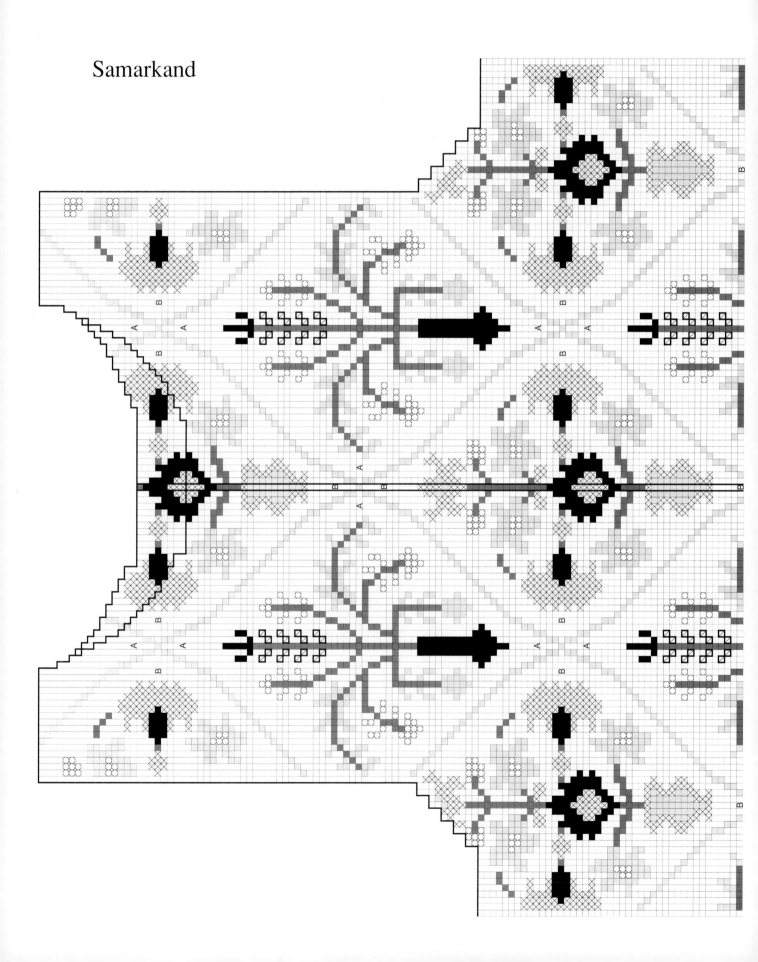

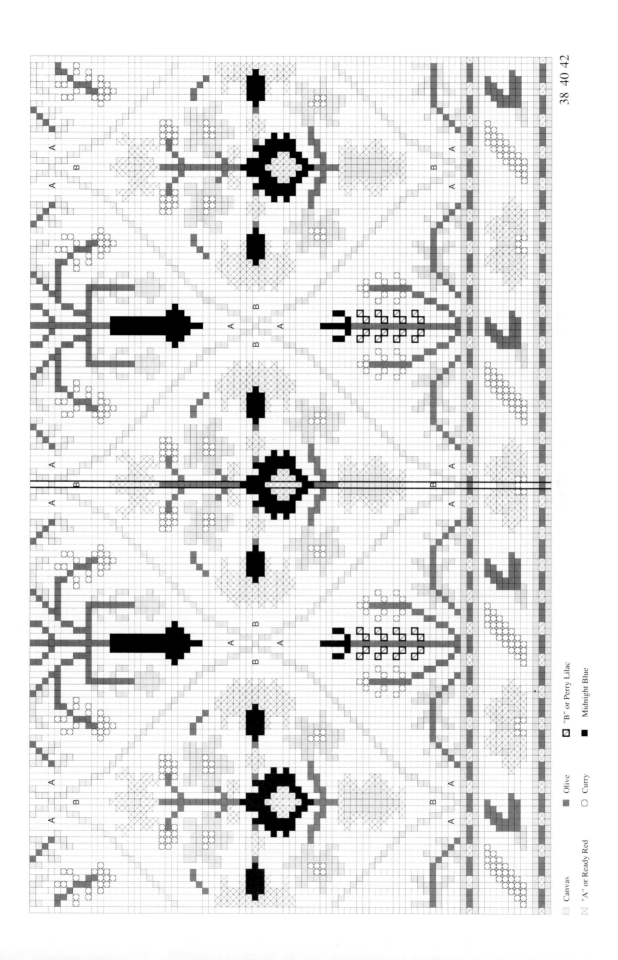

38 40 42

Canvas

"A" or Ready Red

Olive

Curry

"B" or Perry Lilac

Midnight Blue

Marion Hopkins

Late one spring afternoon as I was in the process of writing this book, my husband Charlie, a volunteer ambulance attendant, got a call to bring the ambulance down to Marion Hopkins's house. She was stricken with pneumonia, and the doctor needed assistance in transporting her to the plane. Since we are twelve miles by water from the mainland, one must reach the hospital by plane, lobster boat, or the ferry. After Charlie had been gone about an hour, I heard the familiar rumble of the plane taking off from the airstrip near our house. As I looked out a western window, through the tops of the spruce trees, I saw the plane flying off into the yellow and pink sunset and wondered whether Marion would ever return. She died in the hospital a few days later, and I found myself reflecting on Marion and all of the years we had known each other.

When I moved to this island community twenty years ago, I was a transplanted midwesterner relocated into a stronghold of New England traditions that I didn't understand. My reserved neighbors, who are now very good friends, didn't warm to me immediately, and it was a long, lonely period of becoming accepted and fitting in. Through those first difficult years, Marion, who lived nearby, was always willing to welcome Charlie and me into her home. She often offered to set another place at the table, even though there were already five hungry children taking up the spaces. She always had plenty of stories to tell us or would welcome us into a game of cards or Scrabble. Many cold winter nights were spent visiting with the Hopkins family, and I am sure her friendship is a big part of what pulled us through that difficult transition.

Years later, when I decided to open a yarn shop in town, it was Marion who encouraged me, talked over ideas with me, and showed up every day to run the shop. She waited on customers, taught the novices how to knit, and patiently created sweaters, socks, and hats for those who didn't know which end of the needles to use but had money to spend. Never one to mince words, Marion could always be counted on to tell me exactly what she thought about any situation, and she was always there to remind me, or anyone else, when they began putting on airs. Possessing a tremendous sense of humor, Marion knew every expression ever used on the island and came up with words we had never heard of. When the business moved upstairs as we became a kit company, Marion followed, patiently winding balls all day long. Often I would walk by to find her humming even when she was too tired to stand on her feet, or she would think up some interesting tale to tell us all.

Marion retired a couple of years ago for a much deserved rest. Her children are grown and she had a chance to travel a little, garden, and pursue the many crafts she loved. Whenever I walked into Marion's house by the shore, I always felt surrounded by an abundance of creative ideas. Every room was filled with projects — some barely begun, others half completed, along with many finished ones on display. I always had the feeling that there were many others, only ideas at the moment, waiting to be hatched. For all of her adult years Marion dabbled in crafts — painted boxes, quilted squares, hooked rugs, stuffed animals, painted shells, and "little stupid things," as she described the endless items she fashioned. The one constant creative outlet in her life, since she was taught by a friend in high school, was knitting. She knit socks, mittens, sweaters, and hats, working with every kind of yarn imaginable and often carded, spun, and plied the yarn herself before getting down to knitting a handspun vest or beret.

Marion lived in the house in which she was raised — a traditional island design, a white Cape. When she was first married, she lived down the road in another white house, but after her mother died this Cape again became her home. The view from the dining room table where she always sat looks out to a usually quiet stretch of water, and in the distance Stimpson's Island, which was once inhabited by several families. People rarely live on the smaller islands these days, but Marion could remember the days when they did. Her grandparents used to live on nearby Eagle Island, once teeming with year round residents, now only a summer community. Marion's great uncle

lived there and it was said that he could shear his sheep, card the wool, spin it, and knit it into something useful. A far cry from today, when we would think a man special if he could work with a pair of needles, much less see the project through from start to finish.

As mother of six and grandmother of twelve, Marion knit a considerable number of socks, mittens, and wristers. She and I once tried to guess how many pairs of socks she had constructed in the last 40 years, and decided it had to number somewhere between 500 and 1000. These were rapidly used up by family members, given away as gifts, and occasionally offered already knit for sale. For years, Marion was considered the source of information should you want to learn the craft of sock making. Many a novice knitter has spent an evening at Marion's table being patiently talked through the heel, and several experienced knitters found they needed to return with every sock when that difficult part approached.

Marion never used a pattern and found it difficult to write the directions down, as creating a sock was such an instinctive process for her. She modified sizes in her head and could change from an infant sock to a "full-grown adult foot" with no more than a few moments' thought. Her socks could be colorful or plain. Work socks came in plain gray or natural, or probably whatever yarn cluttered her knitting basket.

Marion Hopkins

Fancy socks were a combination of colors — a toe and heel in colors contrasting with the background was a standard favorite. However the colors are laid out, it is customary to knit an extra strand of reinforcing yarn into the toe and heel. Marion used to use nylon for this, which became difficult to find. More commonly she ended up using a strand of "baby" weight orlon, of a similar or contrasting color to the yarn used in the sock.

Mittens were another knitting staple for Marion with five children's cold hands to be protected during the cold island winters. Occasionally she also knit "wristers," the name given locally to fingerless gloves. These are a perennial favorite for anyone who must work in the cold — whether it be to shingle a house, fish, or go "gunning," a very popular pastime here, especially during the November deer hunting season. These are often knit in blaze orange for the hunters and in gray or any color for those using the mittens for work.

Of course, I learned to knit at Marion's side, starting with socks and eventually graduating to a simple sweater made with bulky weight yarn. As with everything else, Marion was a patient teacher, always willing to explain how to turn a heel one more time, even though we may have tried it the night before. To sit with Marion, it was impossible not to absorb a love of craft whether she was giving a knitting lesson, crafting a funny faced doll or making her traditional Christmas chocolate covered peanut butter balls. I owe to Marion my survival in the community, my start in business, and my introduction to knitting. And, although there are days when I wish I had never seen a pair of needles, I truly can't thank her enough and I will miss her.

Classic Socks

This is a great pattern for experimentation. Use the basic pattern for the shape of the socks,
but choose any color combination – such as the photo (p. 50). The instructions below are written for
Marion's popular two color classic socks.

Sizes: Child's medium, (women's medium, men's large). Directions are for smallest size with larger sizes given in parentheses.
Finished sizes: $6^1/2$ - $7^1/2$ (9-$9^1/2$, 11-$11^1/2$).
Needles: Sizes 3, and 5, double ended, or size needed to obtain gauge of 5.5 sts and 7 rows = 1 inch.
Materials: 1 4 oz. skein MC, 1 2 oz skein.

You want to begin with 34(38,44) sts. With smaller needles and CC loosely cast on the appropriate number of stitches. This is worked in k1, p1 ribbing. I usually knit the ribbing down about 2 to 3 inches. Some prefer to knit the ribbing all the way down to the heel. I see no need of it and besides I hate to knit ribbing. When you finish with the ribbing, increase 2(2,0) sts and change to larger needles and MC. Knit plain until you reach the beginning of the heel. This total distance is according to how tall you want your socks, about six inches for an average woman's sock.

Heel: You will place half of the stitches on one needle. To do this k across 9(10,11) sts on first needle, slip 9(10,11) sts from third needle onto other end of 4th needle. You will now have 18(20,22) sts on heel needle (4th needle). Divide remaining sts on two needles for instep. Now work on heel sts only, with CC. On the first row sl 1, purl across row. On the way back sl 1, k1 across row. That is what makes it double with the "ridgey look." Do this down about 2(2$^1/2$, 3)", ending with a purl row. Now you come to turning the heel, the only tricky part of this whole procedure. Now knit over 9(10,11) sts, then k2 tog, k1, turn. Then sl 1, purl 3, purl 2 tog, purl 1, turn. You will have a little gap on each side where you turned. Always slip lst st. *Sl 1, k4, k2 tog, k1, turn, sl 1, p5, p2 tog, p1, turn. Keep doing this working 1 more st between

decreases until you get to the end. There remain on needle 11(12,13) sts, (knit row).

Instep: With first needle and MC pick up and k 9(10,10) sts on one side of heel. K instep sts to one needle dec 2(2,0) sts evenly spaced. With 3rd needle, pick up and k 9(10,10) sts on other side of heel and with same needle k 5(4,6) from heel needle. To shape instep: 1st rnd; k to within last 3 sts on first needle, k2 tog, k1; k across 2nd needle; on 3rd needle k1, slip, k and pass, k to end of round. 2nd rnd; k around. Repeat last two rounds until 9(10,11) sts remain on each of the first and third needles. K even until foot measures 2 inches less than desired finished length.

Toe: With CC beg at center of sole, knit to within 3 sts of end of first needle, k 2 tog, k1. On 2nd needle, k1, slip 1, k and pass, k to within 3 sts of end, k2 tog, k1. On third needle, k1, sl 1, k and pass, k to end. K 1 round even. Repeat last 2 rounds 6 times; then repeat dec round every round until 12 sts remain. K 3 sts on first needle and slip to 3rd needle. Weave sole and instep sts tog. I usually repeat these two rounds until I have it narrowed down to three or four stitches on each needle. Slip sts evenly to two needles. Break off yarn leaving about 12".

Weaving Toe: Thread end of yarn into tapestry needle and weave sts together as follows: *Pass needle through first st of front needle as if to k and slip st off, pass through 2nd st of front needle as if to p but leave st on needle, draw yarn through; pass needle through first st of back needle as if to p, slip st off, pass needle through 2nd st of back needle as if to k, leave st on needle, draw yarn through; repeat from * until all sts are joined; fasten off. Draw up yarn so that tension of woven sts will be same as knitted sts. Weave in all ends.

Classic Socks

Pam Allen

Like many designers, Pam has been knitting all of her life. She taught herself most of what she knows, although she has strong memories of a German grandmother who would visit once a year. This grandmother would appear wearing elaborate suits and skirts she had knit on very small needles. In high school Pam had a job in the yarn and fabric department of a local store, and this accelerated her growing hobby. Her first projects were plain sweaters, but by the time she was in her twenties, she was collecting yarns and modifying patterns to suit herself. The beginnings of knitting as a career came in the late sixties when she landed a job sewing in a "British Boutique" in her native Chicago. Later she opened her own shop and incorporated knitting into her work by cutting shapes out of knit pieces and sewing them on to the tunics, pants and dresses she was creating.

Pam went on to college, where she studied French, including a year spent in France. While there, she combined her hobby with learning the language by knitting with French knitting books. After she returned to America, Pam spent time working in the publications business, building a house, and having children, but eventually she got back into knitting again. Her first business venture began with a knitting machine, creating colorful sweaters with large, graphic designs out of exotic yarns such as silk and mohair. At this, Pam says that it took two and a half years to make more than two dollars an hour.

Her first break in the designing world came when she shared a taxi with Nora

O'Leary of *Woman's Day* magazine after a New York needlework trade show. After conversing during their ride across the city, Ms. O'Leary suggested Pam send her a design. She did; the magazine bought two and continues to buy patterns Pam creates. *Vogue Knitting* magazine later approached Pam and, after two submissions, they also accepted one of her designs.

The focus of Pam's life is now shared between raising two children and knitting. Both the creativity involved with producing new designs and the actual act of knitting are Pam's passions. A spare room of her pretty Victorian house on a quiet, tree-lined street in a small coastal Maine town is now filled with sample cards, sketches, and swatches as she works out new designs.

Pam begins a design by drawing a picture of what she would like to create on a large piece of newsprint. She then cuts out the shape and works out the design on the paper mock sweater. Then, using a light

Pam Allen

table, she transfers the design from the sweater to graph paper.

This is only the beginning, of course, for once she begins knitting, the sweater colors will be changed and whole new ideas may emerge. As happens in many creative endeavors, Pam may begin with a vision of one product and finish with a sweater entirely different from what she had first imagined. "The fun part is seeing what happens," she says, because often many new ideas flow from this process.

Pam likes to create "enormous, wide sweaters" and describes her favorite structure as "a flat piece — with the body giving it dimension."

"I love to wear sweaters," she comments. "It is fun to create something that feels good to be in." Designing motif sweaters is new; her earlier sweaters focused on geometric and textured patterns. She now pores through books, thinking about new images, and is particularly attracted to the simplicity and clarity of folk art.

Pam works in an upstairs room cluttered with a huge collection of yarns that are a strong source of inspiration. She likes to design where it's quiet, with no distractions, but she knits everywhere, bringing out her latest project every time she sits down for a break. "After my kids, knitting is the most important thing in my life," says Pam, who loves the tactile dimension of knitting — the colors, the warmth, and the needles, as well as the intensity of designing and creating. She describes the creative process for her as a kind of suspension that has its own momentum and is terribly compelling.

"There is a feeling of being energized and relaxed at the same time, a sense of solving problems of your own making. You have a feeling that all is right with the world while you are in this space, and that whatever doubts you will have about a project once it is completed don't exist while the work is being done."

Like all of us, Pam wrestles with her own perfectionism and the difficulties of her work being judged once complete. She agonizes over color choices and the look of the garment until she feels it is just right. In her knitting career she feels that she has had maybe 3 or 4 sweaters that hit on exactly what she wanted. Pam finds making doll sweaters for her daughter very relaxing and when creating these feels she is "less afraid about not being perfect." Designers such as Kaffe Fasset have been a source of inspiration to her, as he throws out concerns about matching dyelots, encourages knitters not to worry about errors, and suggests putting ideas together as one goes along.

Since knitting is an art form women have participated in for centuries, when she's knitting, Pam feels a connection with generations of other women. It may be a connection to ancient women knitting with the fleece of animals we no longer shear or just the simple tie that binds her to her grandmother, knitter of the elaborate skirts. Whatever it is, knitting is firmly grounded in Pam's creative life, and those of us who get to enjoy her designs hope it will always be there for her.

Apples 'n Cream

Sizes: to fit small, medium and large. Directions are for smallest size with larger sizes in parentheses. If there is only one figure it applies to all sizes.

Finished Sizes:
Chest/bust at underarm 38(42,43)"
Length 25$\frac{1}{2}$(26,26$\frac{1}{2}$)"
Sleeve width at upper arm 19(20,20)"

Needles: One pair size 9 needles or size needed to obtain gauge of 17 sts and 23 rows to 4" over stockinette st using size 9 needles.

Materials: 8 4 oz skeins of Lamb's Pride worsted in cream, 1 oz each of light green, dark green, brown, light red, dark red, light blue.

NOTES

(1) SSK decrease (see chart). Sl 2 sts kwise. Insert tip of left needle into fronts of these 2 sts and knit them tog.

(2) Small knot (see chart). Knit into front, back, then front of st. Pass first 2 sts made over last st.

(3) Work the apple tree motif in intarsia, i.e. using a separate strand for each color area making sure not to carry strands for more then 5 sts across back.

(4) Work the yoke in seed st. K1, p1 across row. On the return row, knit the purl sts and purl the knit sts.

(5) The length of the sweater on the chart is 26$\frac{1}{2}$" (large size). To shorten for sizes small and medium, omit rows where indicated.

BACK

Cast on 83 (91, 99) sts in light green. Break off green and attach white. Note: Rows 1-5 are written out below for each size. Starting with Row 6, follow the chart for instructions on the remainder of the sweater, checking notes below for small and medium sizes. It will probably be helpful to follow the chart as well as the written instructions for the first 5 rows.

All Sizes:
Row 1 (WS): Purl

Small Size:
Row 2: K2, p3, *k1, p3, k1, p3, k3, k1, p3, p3; rep. from * 3 more times, end k1, p3, k2.
Row 3: P2, k3, *p1, k3, p1, k3, p3, k3, p1, k3; rep. from * 3 more times, end p1, k3, p2.
Row 4: K2, p3, *k1, p3, k1, p1, p2tog, k1, yo, k1, yo, k1, p2tog, p1, k1, p3; rep from *3 more times, end k1, p3, k2.
Row 5: P2, k3, *p1, k3, p1, k2, p5, k2, p1, k3; rep. from * 3 more times, end p1, k3, p2.

Continue working border by following chart, beg with Row 6, <u>but</u> work first and last 5 sts as follows:
Right side rows: beg k2, p3 and end p3, k2.
Wrong side rows: beg p2, k3 and end k3, p2.

Medium Size:
Row 2: K2, *p3, k1, p3, k1, p3, k1, p3, k3; rep from *3 more times, end p3, k1, p3, k1, p3, k1, p3, k2.
Row 3: P2, *k3, p1, k3, p1, k3, p1, k3, p3; rep from * 3 more times, end k3, p1, k3, p1, k3, p1, k3, p2.
Row 4: K1, *yo, k1, p2tog, p1, k1, p3, k1, p3, k1, p1, p2tog, k1, yo, k1; rep from * 3 more times, end yo, k1, p2tog, p1, k1, p3, k1, p3, k1, p1, p2tog, k1, yo, k1.
Row 5: P3, *k2, p1, k3, p1, k3, p1, k2, p5; rep from * 3 more times, end k2, p1, k3, p1, k3, p1, k2, p3.

Continue working border by following chart, beg with Row 6.

Large Size:
Row 2: K1, p2, *k3, p3, k1, p3, k1, p3, k1, p3; rep from * 4 more times, end k3, p2, k1.
Row 3: p1, k2, *p3, k3, p1, k3, p1, k3, p1, k3; rep from * 4 more times, end p3, k2, p1.
Row 4: k1, p2tog, *k1, yo, k1, yo, k1, p1, p2tog, k1, p3, k1, p3, k1, p1, p2tog; rep

Apples 'n Cream

from *4 more times, end k1, yo, k1, yo, k1, p2tog, k1.

Row 5: p1, k1, *p5, k2, p1, k3, p1, k3, p1, k2; rep from * 4 more times, end p5, k1, p1. Continue working border by following chart, beg with Row 6.
All Sizes:
Row 42: (RS) Purl. (Last row of border).
Small Size:
Skip next 8 rows (43 through 50). Beg st st and continue following chart <u>without</u> working tree motif to Row 132.
Medium Size:
Skip next 4 rows (43-46). Beg st st and continue following chart <u>without</u> working tree motif to Row 132.
Large Size:
Beg working st st on Row 43. Follow chart <u>without</u> working tree motif to Row 132.
All Sizes:
Row 132 (RS): Beg Seed st yoke. Work even in pattern through Row 167. Row 168 (RS): Bind off 27, (30, 33) sts for rt shoulder, leave center 29 (31, 33) sts on holder for back neck, bind off rem 27, (30, 33) sts.

FRONT
Work same as for back through Row 63.
Row 64 (RS): Beg tree motif by following chart and working each color area with a separate strand of yarn.

SHAPE NECK
Row 148 (RS): k36(39,42) sts. Attach a separate ball of yarn. Bind off 11(13,15) sts, work to end of row. Working both sides at once, bind off from each neck edge, 2 sts, then dec <u>every</u> row one st twice, then every other row 5 times. Work 27(30,33) sts of shoulders through Row 167. Row 168: Bind off shoulder sts.

SLEEVES
Cast on 39(43,43) sts in light green. Break yarn and attach white yarn. Work scallop pattern according to chart. Row 16: k2, inc 1, k35(39,39) sts, inc 1 st, k2. Continue in st st inc 1 st, 2 sts in from each edge every 4 rows until there are 81(85,85) sts. Work till sleeve measures 15$\frac{1}{2}$(16,16$\frac{1}{2}$)" from beg. Bind off.

FINISHING
Block pieces. Sew shoulder seams.

NECKBAND
With RS facing, circular needle and white yarn, pick up and k 76 (80, 84) sts evenly around neck edge. Join. Work in k1, p1 rib for 1". Bind off in rib. Place markers 9$\frac{1}{2}$(10,10)" down from shoulders on front and back for armholes. Sew top of sleeves between markers. Sew side and sleeve seams. Work duplicate sts in blue as shown on chart.

Apples 'n Cream

Apples 'n Cream

Front Chart

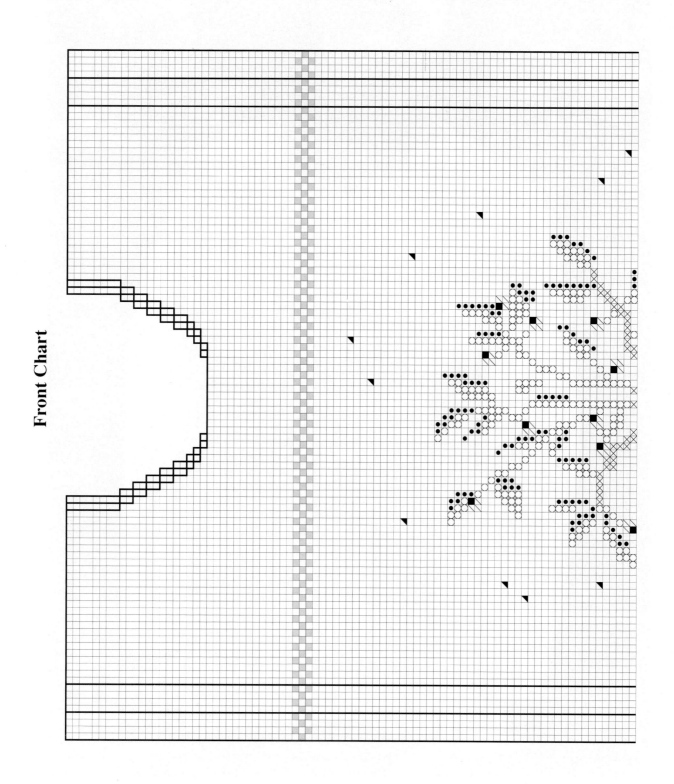

Apples 'n Cream

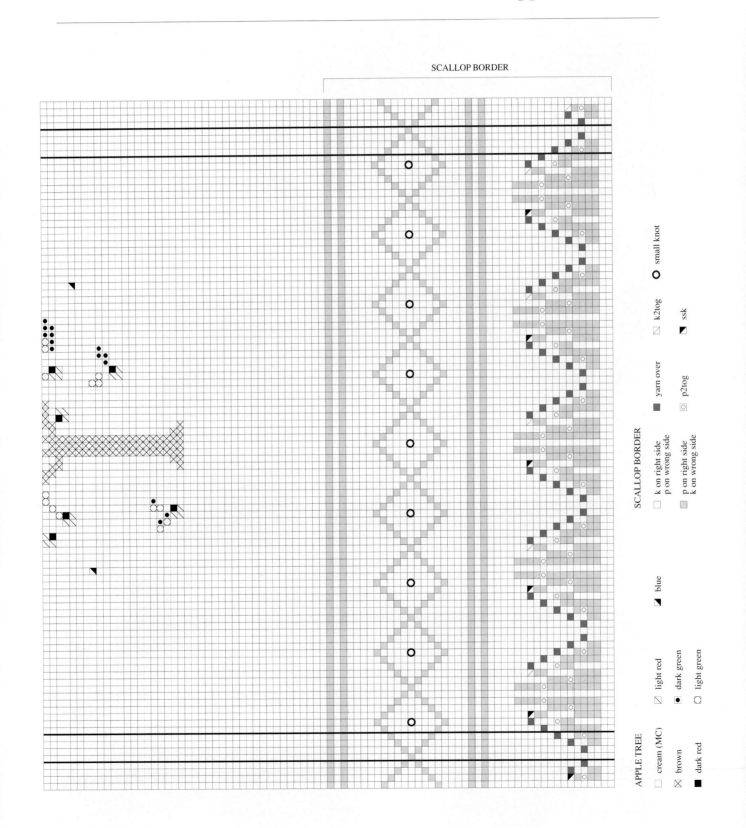

Galloway

Galloway

Sizes: Child sizes 6(8,10,12). Directions are for smallest size with larger sizes in parentheses. If there is only one figure, it applies to all sizes.

Finished Sizes: Finished chest measurement at underarm - 15(16,17,18)". Length - 17(17$\frac{1}{2}$,18$\frac{1}{2}$,20)". Sleeve width at underarm - 6$\frac{1}{2}$(7,7$\frac{1}{2}$,8)".

Needles: One size 7 circular needle - 16" and one pair each sizes 7 and 9 needles or size to obtain gauge of 18$\frac{1}{2}$ sts and 24 rows to 4" over dot pattern using size 9 needles.

Materials: 4 oz. skeins Brown Sheep Farm Lamb's Pride #M63 (Purple Passion) MC
1 4 oz. skein #M64 (Turf Green) A
Small amounts of:
#M59 Periwinkle
#M13 Sun Yellow
#M10 Cream
#M05 Onyx
#M52 Spruce
#M80 Blue Blood Red
#M90 New Dune
#M21 Hot House Pink
Tropical Turquoise
Ruby Lith

BACK

With smaller needles and A, cast on 72 (76,80,84) sts. Rib row 1 (RS) P2 A, *k2 MC, p2 A; rep from *, end k2 MC. Rib row 2 P2 MC, *k2 A, p2 MC; rep from *, end k2 A. Rep last 2 rib rows for 2", end with a WS row. Change to larger needles and with A, k next 2 rows. Following Chart 1, work 4 rows of border pattern and begin dot pattern. Cont. in dot pattern as established until piece measures 15$\frac{3}{4}$ (16$\frac{1}{4}$,17$\frac{1}{4}$,18$\frac{3}{4}$)" from beg, ending WS row. Work 6 rows of Chart 2. Next row (shape shoulder tab): Bind off 54 (56,58,60) sts, inc 1 st by knitting into st below, k13, bind off rem 5 (7,9,11) sts. Join yarn to tab sts and work 3 more rows in A. Bind off.

FRONT

Using smaller needles and A, cast on 72 (76,80,84) sts. Rib row 1 (RS) K2 MC, *p2 A, k2 MC; rep from *, end p2 A. Rib row 2 k2 A, *p2 MC, k2 A; rep from *, end p2 MC. Rep last 2 rib rows for 2", end with a WS row. Change to larger needles and with A, k next 2 rows. Following Chart 1, work 4 rows of border pattern and begin dot pattern. Work dot pattern as established until 6 (7,8,9) rows of dots (not dot pattern) have been worked. With MC only, work 2 more rows. Next row: Work 18 (20,22,24) sts in dot pattern. Work 37 sts of Row 1 of chart for Galloway. Finish row in dot pattern. Work next 40 rows of Galloway chart keeping dot pattern on either side as established. Then work even in dot pattern until piece measures 14$\frac{1}{2}$(15,16,17$\frac{1}{2}$)" from beg, ending WS row.

NECK SHAPING

Work 29 (31,32,34) sts in pattern. Join 2nd ball of MC and bind off center 14 (14,16,16) sts, work to end. Working both sides at once, dec 1 st at each neck edge every other row 10 times. When same length as back, work chart 2 and shape left shoulder tab and make buttonholes as follows: Bind off 5 (7,9,11) sts k3, yo, k2tog, k3, yo, k2tog, k4. When same length as back, bind off 19 (21,22,24) st for right shoulder. Shape left shoulder tab and make buttonholes as follows: (RS) Bind off 5 (7,9,11) sts. K3, yo, k2 tog, k3, yo, k2tog, k4. Work 3 more rows over tab sts and bind off.

Galloway

SLEEVES:
With smaller needles and A, cast on 34 (34,38,38) sts. Rib row 1 (RS) P3 A, *k2 MC, p2 A; rep from *, end k3 MC. Rib row 2 P3 MC, *k2 A, p2 MC; rep from *, end k3 A. Rep last 2 rib rows for 2". Change to larger needles and with A knit 1 row, inc 4 sts evenly spaced across - 38(38,42,42) sts. K next row. Following Chart 1, work 4 rows of border pattern and begin dot pattern, *at same time,* inc 1 st each end every other row 0 (2,3,4) times, then every 4th row 11(11,11,12) times - 60(64,70,74) sts. Work even until piece measures 10(10$\frac{1}{2}$,11,11$\frac{1}{2}$)" from beg. Work 6 rows of Chart 2. Bind off.

FINISHING:
Block pieces. Sew right shoulder seam and left shoulder seam from tab to shoulder. *Neckband:* With RS facing, circular needle and A, pick up and k97(97,101,101) sts around neck edge. K next row. Rib row 1 and buttonhole row (RS) P1 A, p2tog, yo in A, *k2 MC, p2 A; rep from *, ending k2 MC. Rib row 2 P2 MC, *k2 A, p2 MC; rep from * end k3 A. Rep the last 2 rows once. Knit one row in A. Bind off in A. Sew sleeves to body and sew side and sleeve seams. Sew buttons opposite buttonholes on shoulder.

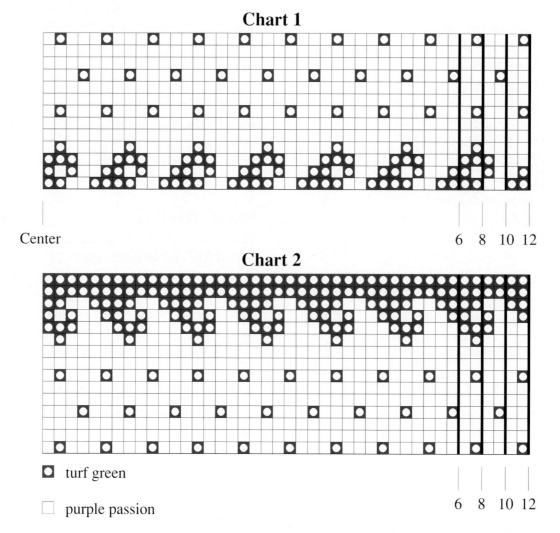

Chart 1

Center   6 8 10 12

Chart 2

☐ turf green   6 8 10 12

☐ purple passion

Galloway

Chart 3

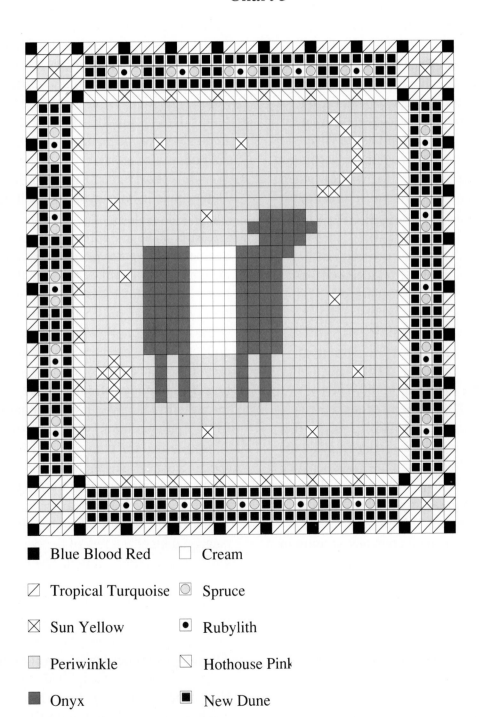

■	Blue Blood Red	□	Cream
⧄	Tropical Turquoise	◎	Spruce
⊠	Sun Yellow	⊡	Rubylith
▨	Periwinkle	⧅	Hothouse Pink
▨	Onyx	■	New Dune

Hélène Rush

There's usually a lot of activity at the Rush household, and most often Hélène is at the center of it. The day I came by to visit, the family was having an above-ground pool installed in the backyard of their busy, suburban home that backs up to a quiet patch of woods. There were dogs barking, children running in and out of the house, and workmen knocking on the door, borrowing hair dryers and vacuums to help them finish the job. When I asked Hélène how she was going to avoid the constant lure of the pool just outside of the window when she needs to knit on those hot summer days, she said, "I'll just start early and work late." After seeing all that she has accomplished, I am sure she will.

Hélène Rush was the only knitter I spoke with who actually said she learned to knit in school. A French-Canadian raised in Montreal, she said that knitting was part of her school's home economics curriculum and all girls were taught to knit. (She didn't know what the boys did — "probably watched TV.") She remembers creating a garter stitch potholder, a dickey, and scarf and, most important, she remembers that all the girls took their work home and got a little help from their mothers. Cheating? Maybe, but probably a great way to keep families involved in the craft of knitting.

Hélène was in good company knitting in her home, as she grew up in a very creative household. Her mother was a seamstress and her father "made and fixed everything," including a tartan plaid coat for the family dog — complete with a fleece lining.

Creativity rubbed off on Hélène who was able to make sweaters without a pattern while still a teenager. Hélène gives the credit for her start as a designer to one of the other designers in this book, Dot Ratigan. When Dot was running her yarn shop, Hélène stopped by. She noticed an article posted in the shop that described Dot's design work and decided to try submitting a few patterns to various companies herself. Creating from her own ideas, she knit some sweaters and sent them out to magazines and yarn companies. After many rejection letters, Hélène finally sold three designs to *Ladies' Circle* magazine. After this, she sold designs to a yarn company, then to *Woman's World* magazine and others. As Hélène puts it, "once you start selling, it seems to keep moving."

After Hélène's third child was born, she decided to leave her job and take up her design work full-time. Along with free-lance designing, Hélène has also written four books. The most well known of these is the first, *Maine Woods Woolies* — a collection of sweaters for children with such distinctly Maine motifs as puffins, light-houses and moose. Hélène wrote, provided the patterns, and even took the photographs for this popular book, which has sold over 30,000 copies since it was published in 1985. She now has contracts for two more books and is busily trying to find time to finish the patterns for them.

Not content to just design, Hélène also packaged kits for a few of her designs and wrote a newsletter entitled, *The Knitting Gazette*.

It is a good thing Hélène is young because she juggles many tasks at one time. She says that in the six years she has been designing at home she has never quite been caught up. A very disciplined worker, Hélène puts in as many hours now as she did when she worked at a nine-to-five desk job, patterns, and plenty of useful advice garnered from her years with the needles.

It is a good thing Helene is young because she juggles many tasks at one time. She says that in the six years she has been designing at home she has never quite been caught up. A very disciplined worker, Helene puts in as many hours now as she did when she worked at a nine to five desk job, and usually many more. She often sends out as many as two or three designs a week and tries never to say no to any request from the long list of magazines and yarn companies that she works with.

Her work begins when she receives a call or letter from a yarn company about to market a new yarn or magazine describing a plan for a coming issue. The request for a design may be a very specific or it may only suggest a vague theme and the kind of yarn to be used. Helene then goes to work, submitting a sketch of the garment she has planned, as well as a knitted swatch of the main motif or pattern stitch of the sweater. If accepted, she will complete the design and provide the company with a knitted sweater to photograph. To keep up with her work load, Helene often has other knitters help make the simpler sweaters, although she knits the most complicated garments herself. Like most other knitters, she is never far away from her needles when the TV is on or during any other idle moment.

Helene has learned that she has to be flexible. Her feeling is that if your attitude is, "Nobody is going to touch my work," you won't get very far. She finds that a designer must be very accommodating, must get used to editors making changes and also get desensitized to rejection. If Helene

sends ten ideas to an editor and one is accepted, she considers that very good.

As Helene put it, "I should have two lives." Even that might not give her time to pursue all of the things she is interested in doing. A lover of many crafts besides knitting, Helene is trying to talk herself out of joining a quilting club, because she just doesn't have time, but she hates to pass up the opportunity. She also loves woodworking and showed me some of the furniture she has built for her home including the cupboard doors with stained glass inserts she is working on. Then there are the three kids and their friends, all waiting for a snack.... An idle moment? Don't look for it in this very busy designer's home.

Plaid Flower Cardigan

A colorful channel type jacket in short length. The motifs used are very folkloric looking and although 4 colors are worked at once, the use of duplicate stitch makes it simpler.

Sizes: 36(38,40,42)
Finished Bust Size: 39(41,43,45)
Needles: One pair size 8 needles or size to obtain correct gauge in St st, 4.5 sts and 6 rows = 1". One size J crochet hook. Bobbins and tapestry needle.
Materials: Worsted weight 85% wool/15% mohair (4 ounces/190 yards skein): 4 (4-5-5) skeins color creme (A), 2 skeins each color onyx (B) and spruce (C). 1 skein blue blood red (D). 6 buttons.

NOTES
For best results, work colors B and C only for rows 7-29 of color chart working colors A and D later in duplicate stitch. For last 20 rows of chart, work a "purl" groove in background color where indicated with "P", use bobbins for color C and duplicate stitch for color D.

BACK
With B cast on 85(91,95,99) sts. Work following color chart repeating last 20 rows for rest of back. At 19(20,21,22)" from beg, work across 29(31,33,34) sts, leave on holder for shoulder, bind off next 27(29,29,31) sts for back of neck, work across rem sts and leave on holder for shoulder.

LEFT FRONT
With B, cast on 43(46,48,50) sts. Work color placement as for back. At the same time, at $16^1/_2$ ($17^1/_2$,$18^1/_2$,$19^1/_2$)" from beg.
Shape Neck: Wrong side facing, bind off 10(11,11,12) sts and complete row. Then, dec 1 st at neck edge every other row 4 times - 29(31,33,34) sts. Work even until same length as back to shoulder. Leave sts on holder.

RIGHT FRONT
Work as for left front reversing chart and neck shaping.

SLEEVES
With B, cast on 49(49,55,55) sts. Work following color chart repeating last 20 rows for rest of sleeve. At the same time, inc 1 st each end every 1" 14(16,15,17) times working color pattern on new sts - 77(81,85,89) sts. Work even until 16($16^1/_2$,17,$17^1/_2$)" from beg. Bind off all sts.

FINISHING
Knit shoulder sts tog (see knitted seam method diagram). With crochet hook and B, starting at front, work chain stitch in "P" groove going up over the shoulders, and down back. Repeat for each sleeve. Fill in all extra colors in duplicate stitch where needed. Weave in all ends. Measure $8^1/_2$ ($9,9^1/_2$,10)" on each side of shoulder seams and place markers on armhole edge. Set in sleeves between markers. Sew underarm and side seams.

CROCHET BANDS
Attach yarn at left shoulder seam. Round 1: With crochet hook and B, ch 1, and work around entire edge of neck, fronts and bottom in sc working 3 sc at each corner ending with sl st to ch 1 at beg. Round 2: Ch 1, work even in sc omitting "3 sc"

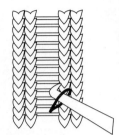
increase in corners. Round 3: Work as for round 1 evenly spacing 6 "ch-2" buttonloops in right front band having top and bottom ones $1/2$" from edge. Round 4: Work as round 2 making 2 sc in "ch-2" space from previous row. Round 5: Work as for round 1. Fasten off. Sew buttons opposite buttonholes. For sleeves, attach yarn at seam. Ch1, work 34(34,38,38) sc around edge ending with sl st to ch 1 at beg. Repeat this round 4 times more. Fasten off.

CHAIN STITCH IN "P" GROOVE

Insert hook through fabric in first row of "P" indicated on chart. Draw yarn through fabric leaving one loop on hook. Insert hook 2 rows higher, draw yarn through fabric and through loop on hook to form chain. Repeat this last step every 2 rows.

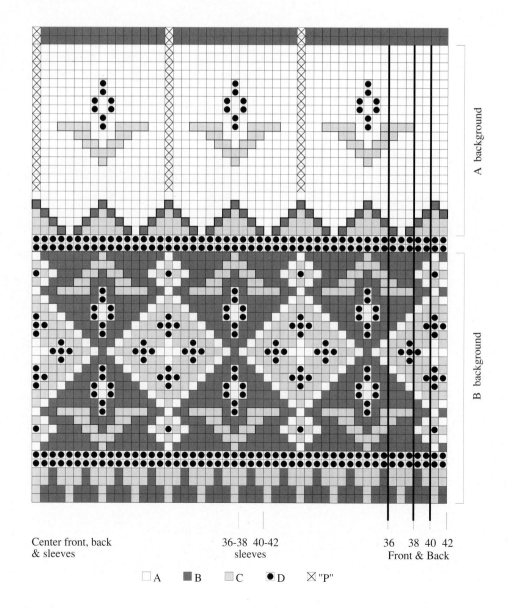

A background

B background

Center front, back & sleeves

36-38 40-42
sleeves

36 38 40 42
Front & Back

☐A ■B ☐C ●D ☒"P"

Plaid Flower Cardigan

Susie Hanson

On a shelf in the kitchen, Susie Hanson keeps a message she saved from a fortune cookie. It says, "You will be very successful in business." After getting to know Susie, I had to agree — she will.

Last year Susie started her own home-based company, S. M. Hanson Designs, marketing Christmas stocking kits. She had been designing, knitting, and giving stockings away for birthday, Christmas, and even wedding presents for years, and eventually got the idea to make them available as kits for others to knit. Over the past four years, Susie estimates she has knit 250 of these stockings, and in the first nine months of business she sold about 750 kits to knitting stores from Maine to California.

Susie has been a prolific knitter for most of her life. She has a comfortable chair in the corner of her living room, and next to it sits a basket of yarn and her latest projects. After putting in a long day meeting the needs of her business, along with tending to her two small children, she sits down in the chair. Usually she doesn't get up until 1 a.m., when she heads to bed after completing an average of nine hours of knitting throughout the day. No project is too difficult for Susie, who even knit her wedding dress. The day I visited, she was working on a coat for her niece that was similar to 15 she had already knit and sold.

As a child in Wisconsin, Susie learned to knit from her Swedish grandmother, who would put the stitches on the needle and Susie and her sister would take it from there. After countless scarves, Susie took on a fisherman-knit sweater for her first project, and there was very little she wouldn't tackle after that. She grew up on a horse farm and was active in 4H, where she enhanced her knitting skills. In college she studied interior design, although she says she did more knitting than studying. She had been working at a variety of different jobs when a family member encouraged her to quit, stay home, and turn her knitting into a career.

She says that knitting reminds her of those moments with her grandmother and, although she is long gone, makes Susie feel close to her again. It has helped her through another difficult time as well — when Susie was twenty-six she discovered that she had breast cancer, the same disease to which she lost her mother at forty-eight. She credits knitting as "the only thing that kept me relaxed during the treatments," and says without it her "fingernails would have been chewed down to the knuckle." Her four-year-old son Bryce was born a year after her treatments. Although Susie and her doctors were nervous about her pregnancy, he was born perfectly healthy.

Susie faced cancer again two years after the first round, and it gave her a chance to learn a great deal about her community. As a midwesterner moving into a coastal Maine town, Susie had been struck by the differences in the regions and found that her neighbors had a tendency to make distinctions between those who were native and those "from away." After being sick, there was no question that she belonged to this

Susie Hanson

community, and she was touched by the outpouring of support. People brought in lobsters and food and helped take care of her and her family in many ways. Through her illness she got to know many people — in fact, when they had Jack (their adopted son) christened, over 100 people came. Susie gives credit to the support of her friends and family and her own positive attitude for getting her through all of those difficult times. She feels she is tougher now and doesn't "get walked on," and there is no question that she appreciates her life.

Working at home is one of the ways she enjoys her life now. There is time to be with the two boys and to do what she loves. She sells several different stocking kits with motifs ranging from Christmas themes, such as holly and gingerbread men, to the Maine favorites of lobsters and sailboats. She got her start in wholesaling from her sister-in-law, who showed her stockings to a yarn shop in Michigan that ordered ten kits. When they placed a second order, she knew she was on to something.

So she put together a simple brochure with some photos and sent them out to 200 yarn shops she found listed in a magazine. Then Susie, who seems to know people all over the country, hit on the idea of asking her friends and family to photocopy the yarn shop sections of their local yellow pages and send them to her. A helpful relative in Northern California sent a lot of pages, making that one of Susie's best territories.

Like many designers turned entrepreneur, Susie has gone through the usual difficulties of getting perspective on customer complaints, even though they may be few. After the first letter she sat down and had a good cry, and then wrote the customer a letter discussing her criticism. She's learning not to take these things personally but to remember that knitting is not an exact science and everyone always has what they think is a better idea.

Expanding the business while keeping it within the range that she and her family can handle is a challenge. Son Bryce, at four and a half, is his mom's right-hand man. He helps her wind the balls of yarn, packs the boxes, and meets the UPS man. All of this causes Susie to joke that the "S. M." in the company name stands for "son and mom." Her husband, who "used to complain about her knitting until it started to make money," now helps out and has gone from calling it "her pretend business" to "our business."

Susie has now expanded to a line of children's sweaters and finds her inspiration for design all around her. When she gets together with friends or family members, they start talking about good ideas. Before Susie leaves one of these knitting "jam sessions," she has a plan and then goes home and puts it together. She'll start the design by graphing it and getting all of her yarns out on the kitchen table to choose what would work best. After knitting begins, she rips and rips until she has what she likes. She still knits a considerable number of stockings for her wholesale customers to display and for sale at local craft fairs for $40. She also knits a wide variety of custom motifs and has recently done one with teeth for a dentist.

In spare moments, Susie and her husband often work on the house she designed and they built together. In the summer they like to spend their time out in boats. They have a small sailboat and recently they refinished a "Lyman Islander Classic," which they will use for family outings and fishing. Susie loves to entertain and cook for people; she loves her work and being with her family. There is no question about it, Susie just loves life. With an attitude like that, I don't think she can possibly fail.

Tulips

Sizes: 2(4,6,8,10,12) Actual chest measurements: 20(22,24,26,28,30)"

Finished Sizes: Chest Measurements: 22(24, 26,28,30,32) When only one number is given it applies to all sizes.

Needles: One set size 4 and 7 single-pointed needles or size needed to obtain gauge of 5 sts = 1 inch using larger needles. One 16" circular needle size 5, stitch holders and markers.

Materials: Bartlett Yarns Homespun Worsted Weight Yarn -
Black 6(8,10) oz (MC)
Emerald 3 oz
2 oz of each: Iris, Scarlet, Royal Blue, Cranberry and Maize.

BACK

With smaller needles and MC, cast on 56(60,66,70,74,80) sts. Work in k1, p1 ribbing for 1(1^1/2,2,2,2,2)" increasing 3(3,1,1,1,1) sts evenly on last row of ribbing. With 59(63,67,71,75,81) sts on needle, change to larger needles and with MC work next 2 rows in st st (knit 1 row, purl 1 row). Next row (RS): follow chart 1 until piece measures 8(9,10,10^1/2,11,12)" or desired length to underarm. Place marker through last st on each end to mark beginning of underam. Continue working chart 1 for another 6(6,6^1/2,7,7,7^1/2)". End with a purl row. Place first 13(15,16,18,19,22) sts on a holder. Place center 33(33,35,35, 37,37) sts on a second holder. Place remaining 13(15,16,18,19,22) sts on a third holder.

FRONT

Work as back until armhole measures 3(3, 3^1/2,4,4,4^1/2)". End having just purled a row.

NECK SHAPING

Continue working chart 1 while shaping neck, k 16(18,19,21,22,25), k2tog, sl center 23(23,25,25,27,27) sts to a holder. Join second ball of yarn, sl 1,k1, psso, work to end. Next row purl even across. Continue to dec at neck edge every k row 4 times more. (5 times total) 13(15,16,18,19,22) sts rem each side. Work armhole until piece measures same as back. Sl sts to a holder.

SLEEVES

With smaller needles and MC, cast on 36(38,38,40,42,44) sts. Work in k1, p1, ribbing for 1(1^1/2,2,2,2,2)". Inc 6(6,8,8,8,8) sts evenly across last row of ribbing, 42(44,46,48,50,52) sts on needle. Change to larger needles and with MC, work next 2 rows in st st. Next row: follow chart 2 inc 1 st each side every 6th row 7(7,8,9,9,10) times. 56(58,62,66,68,72) sts on needle. Work until sleeve measures 10(11,12,13, 14,15)" or desired lehgth. Bind off sts loosely.

FINISHING

Join shoulder sts using the knitted seam method. Sew sleeves between markers. Sew side seams.

NECKBAND

With circular needle and MC, starting at back of neck, k 33(33,35,35,37,37) sts from back holder. Pick up and knit 8 sts along neck edge. K 23(23,25,25,27,27) sts from front holder. Pick up and k8 sts along neck edge, 72 (72,76,76,76,76) on needle. Work in k1, p1 rib for 5 rows. Bind off loosely.

Tulips

Tulips

Chart 1

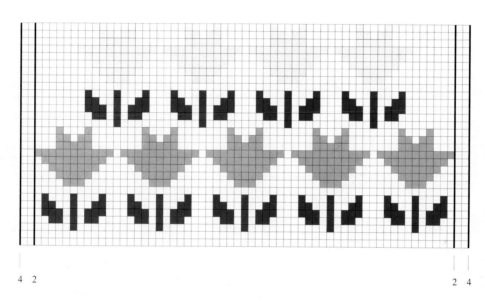

4 2   2 4

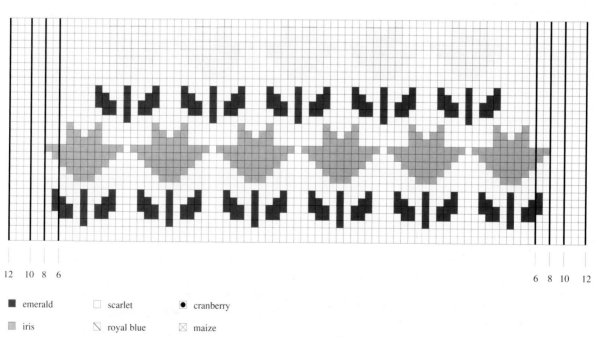

12 10 8 6   6 8 10 12

■ emerald   □ scarlet   ● cranberry

■ iris   ◺ royal blue   ⊠ maize

Tulips

Chart 2

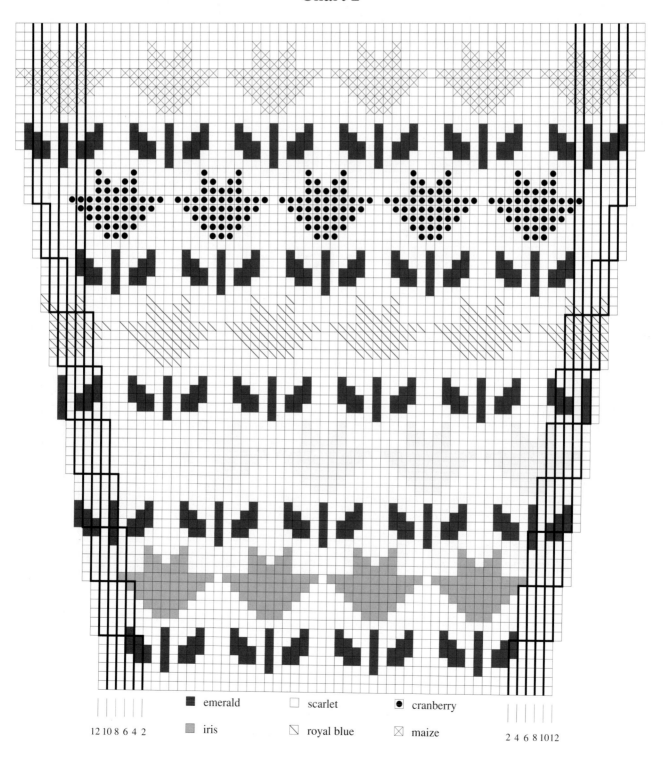

■ emerald   □ scarlet   ● cranberry

▨ iris   ◫ royal blue   ⊠ maize

Jean White

For seven years, Jean White and I were neighbors on this small island while her husband served as superintendent/principal of our school. Our children were friends, and we shared an occasional cup of tea and compared notes on our adopted community. There was never a time when I walked into the Whites' busy house on the main street in town and did not find evidence of a knitting project. Often Jean would display her latest sweaters on the family's round dining table, excitedly showing me through the pile of beautiful textures and styles knit in wonderful tweeds and colors. It was evident, even as Jean explained the designs to a non-knitter like me, that these were exciting patterns and this was a passionate knitter.

Jean knit countless custom designed sweaters for our yarn shop customers and brought quantities more down to sell on the consignment table. She and her family are now living hundreds of miles from the island, in a northern Maine town in the area where she and her husband both grew up. In spite of our distance, we still occasionally receive boxes of Jean's lovely sweaters, and their arrival is always greeted with excitement by all who work here.

Growing up, Jean learned the basics from her mother — a "wonderful knitter"— who would tackle any sweater as long as she had a pattern. Jean, on the contrary, never learned to read a pattern when she was young, so began knitting by copying what she saw. Thus her current style developed, that of making sweaters as easy and logical to knit as possible, while still producing a garment that looks complicated.

A very knowledgeable knitter, Jean also understands the origins of the garments she knits. For instance, while we were discussing Guernsey sweaters, one of her specialties, she informed me that these close-fitting designs essentially started out as undershirts. Just as T-shirts have come to be outerwear in our culture, so the Guernsey became used as a warm outer sweater years ago.

According to Jean, Fair Isle and Lopi designs, both of which incorporate their patterns into the yoke of the garment, represented a thrifty use of multicolored yarns into an area least likely to be covered by a fisherman's overalls. The double stranding in a pattern also served to concentrate the warmth into certain areas of a sweater where it was especially needed.

Jean is an avid reader and always has been intrigued by a wide variety of subjects. She began broadening her horizons early. At the young age of 15, influenced by a schoolteacher from England, she became very interested in the culture of Great Britain. She proposed to her father that she leave her rural Maine home and spend a year in a British school. Her father didn't believe that she would achieve her goal, but he agreed, providing that she "be accepted by a good school, find a place to live, and pay her own way." Jean managed to accomplish all three and ended up doing so well in school that she stayed through her high school years and into three years of college.

During her stay in England, Jean was able to observe the diverse European traditions of knitting and the wide variety of patterns, styles, and yarns. Perhaps more important, she was also able to develop an "intellectual appreciation for arts and crafts, as well as a practical enjoyment of them." It is this thoughtful appreciation that is so evident in the patterns she creates and the satisfaction she derives from her work.

Jean enjoys knitting classic patterns and concentrates on the textured relief of Guernseys and Arans and the multi-color knitting of Fair Isle and Nordic sweaters. She is pleased that the sweaters she knit twenty years ago are still fashionable and comfortable today, and

Jean White

looks forward to the sweaters she is creating today being as long-lived.

Along with her love of the classic she has a strong desire to "figure out how to make the complicated uncomplicated." She does this by using such tricks as "visual memories" — easily learned stitches that will appear on the outer edge of each row in a routine manner or in simple units of pattern within a sweater. As these are completed, they remind the knitter to do something in the more complex design units such as "when two of these squares are knit, then I turn the cable." Jean likes patterns that are symmetrical, where "the eye and brain can work in concert."

"Doodling with yarn," is Jean's way of working out patterns. She also often charts her patterns on paper before she starts to knit, playing with the patterns to get them to come out right. One of her pet peeves is a "design element being interrupted by a structural detail," and she works hard to make sure that never happens.

Jean knits about thirty sweaters a year, about one every two weeks. Like many knitters, she says that every time she sits down, it is never without knitting in her hands. She wonders if it is the "puritanical" side of her, wanting to be sure that she has "led a useful life," that keeps her busy with the craft. More than that, Jean finds knitting to be "relaxing and therapeutic" both for the tactile and intellectual stimulation and the feeling of accomplishment upon finishing an attractive, functional project. As with most other designers, her nemesis is the use of poor yarn. She is a true lover of beautiful yarns favoring wool, and wool blended with mohair, alpaca, or silk.

Knitting is not Jean's only creative outlet — she has been quilting as long as she has been knitting, and she also sews, does traditional rug hooking, and restores rugs and quilts. Jean has taught classes in all of these things and written articles for *Threads*, *Lady's Circle Patchwork Quilts*, and *Knitting World*, with other articles in progress. These activities are worked around her busy schedule, which often includes teaching both high school students and adults, gardening, and managing a household that includes five children.

What is Jean's goal as someone who teaches knitting through classes and patterns? She says that, after her years of deciphering this sometimes complicated process, she would like to be able to pass on several ideas to other knitters. One is that "they are in charge, instead of the pattern." Further, she would give knitters the idea that they can think through a pattern logically, and when they come across a problem, they should have the confidence to determine that the problem may have been with the pattern, not with them. After many years of watching her simplify this craft, I have to admit — Jean is beginning to make knitting look pretty easy, even to a novice like me.

Boatman

Somewhat oversized, this heavily textured, drop-shoulder, unisex sweater is for the confident intermediate knitter. Once your brain and eyes see how the various designs develop, you will rarely need to refer to the charts, so logical is the knitting.

Sizes: 38(40,42)
Finished Sizes: 40(43,46)"
Underarm Body Length: 16$\frac{1}{2}$(17$\frac{1}{4}$,19$\frac{1}{2}$)"
Underarm Sleeve Length: (allowing for extra length gained by dropped shoulder) 17$\frac{1}{2}$(18$\frac{1}{4}$,19)"
Needles: Size 7 and 9 for sizes 38 and 40, gauge of 3$\frac{3}{4}$ sts, 5$\frac{1}{2}$ rows = 1 inch over stockinette stitch; size 8 and 10 for size 42, 3$\frac{1}{2}$ sts, 5 rows = 1 inch; 16" circular size 8.
Materials: 7(8,8) skeins

BACK

With smaller needles, cast on 70(72,72) sts. Work in k1, p1, ribbing for 2$\frac{1}{4}$(2$\frac{3}{4}$,2$\frac{3}{4}$)", ending with a wrong-side row just completed. Knit across front using larger needles, increasing evenly to 74(80,80)" sts. Work 3(4,4) garter st ridges by knitting the next 6(8,8) rows. Purl 1 row.
Panel 1: Follow and complete panel 1. Purl 1 row, knit 7 rows, purl 1 row.
Panel 2: Work Panel 2, then purl across next row. Knit 7 rows, purl 1 row.
Panel 3: Work Panel 3. Knit 7 rows, purl 1 row.
Panel 4: Complete Panel 4, purl next row, then knit 7 rows.
Panel 5: Work 5th panel, then knit 10 rows. Bind off all sts purlwise. When you break off the yarn, leave 20" attached to the work to be used for sewing the shoulders together later.

FRONT

Work exactly as for the back until you are on the last row of panel 5. Work 27(30,30) sts of that row; bind off center 20 sts; work last 27(30,30) sts. Knit the next 10 rows of each shoulder, decreasing 1 st at neck edge every other row 5 times, leaving 22(25,25) sts per shoulder before binding off purlwise, leaving 20" of yarn attached as before.

Press wrong side of work lightly, measuring carefully as you do so to ensure that pieces are of the correct dimensions. A real advantage of using good wool is that you can coax your work into shape easily, without damaging it! Make sure selvedges are nice and smooth to ensure easy sewing later.

SHOULDER SEAMS

Place front and back pieces together, right sides facing. The bound-off edges will seem slightly beveled towards each other: sew the seams by catching the upper loops of the bound off sts using the length of yarn previously left attached. This will create an attractive finish in which the join itself is virtually invisible from the right side of the work.

SLEEVES

Using larger needles, and with the right side of the work facing you, pick up 74(80,80) sts from the front and back armhole areas, beginning and ending about 1$\frac{2}{3}$" (1", 1") up from the start of panel 4. To get this number, you will need to pick up approx 3 sts for every 4 rows of body knitting. Knit 6 rows to make 3 garter ridges, and then start charted design on a wrong side row. Decrease 1 st at the start of the 4th and 5th rows (slip 1, work 2nd st, pass slipped st

Boatman

over), and continue thus until 46 sts remain, and 4 full repeats of the center diamond have been made. Work 3(4,4) garter st ridges, and then change to smaller needles to make cuff. On 1st row of the k1, p1 ribbing, decrease evenly to 38(38,40) sts and then continue on these sts until cuff is desired depth ($2^1/2$" to $3^1/2$"). Bind off loosely in ribbing, that is, knitting the k sts, purling the p sts as you come to them, before binding them off.

SEAMS
Again, press work lightly from wrong side. Sew side and underarm seams together, and work in any ends of yarn there might be.

NECK
With circular needle, pick up an even number of sts (approx 70 - 76 is a good range) and work a k1, p1 rib for 6($6^1/2$, 7)". Bind off loosely in ribbing.

PANEL 1

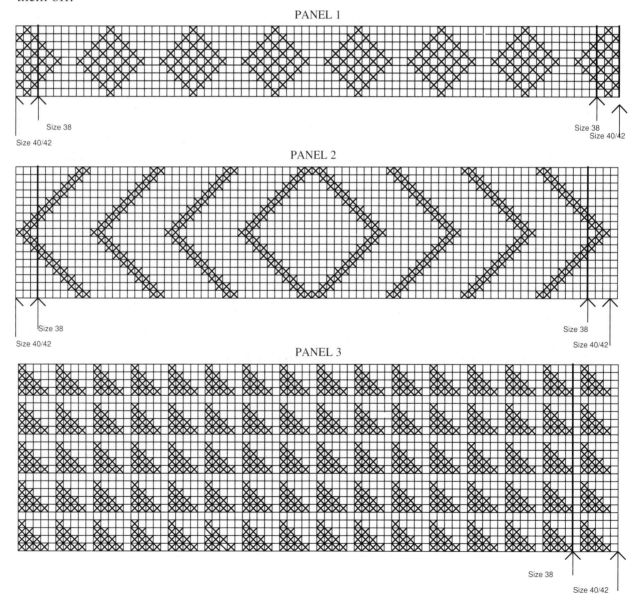

PANEL 2

PANEL 3

Boatman

PANEL 4

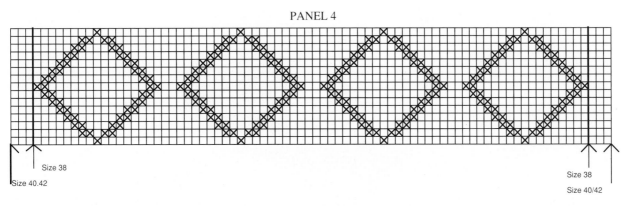

Size 38

Size 40.42

Size 38

Size 40/42

PANEL 5

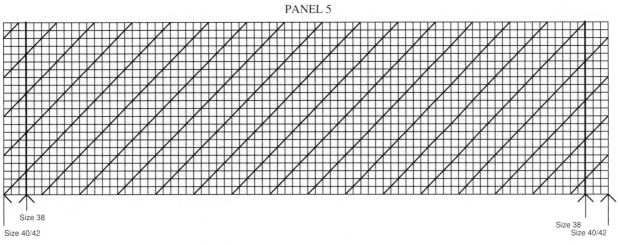

Size 38

Size 40/42

Size 38
Size 40/42

SLEEVE

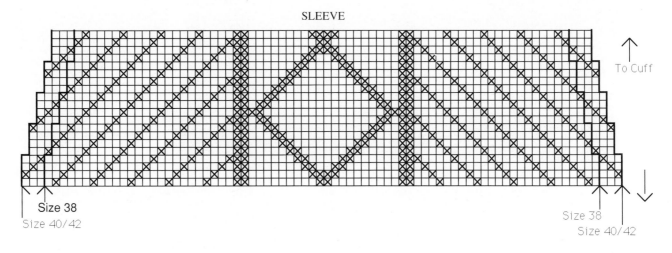

To Cuff

Size 38

Size 40/42

Size 38

Size 40/42

A ☑ or ☒ means purl on right side of work and knit on wrong side.

Boatman

Cables and Diamonds

Cables and Diamonds

Moderately oversized, this sweater is for the intermediate knitter who wishes to practice basic relief stitches.

Sizes: 38(40,42)"
Finished Sizes: 41(43,45)"
Underarm Body Length: 17^1/2(18^1/4,19)"
Underarm Sleeve Length: 18(18^1/2,18^1/2)"
Needles: 1 cable needle; size 7, 10" or size needed to obtain stitch gauge of 4 sts and 5 rows = 1" using larger needles over body pattern; 16" circular size 8
Materials: 7(8,8) skeins

BACK
With smaller needles, cast on 81(87,93) sts. Work in k1, p1, ribbing for 3". Change to larger needles and begin body, repeating these 4 rows:
   Row 1: K, Row 2: P, Row 3: K,
   Row 4: K1, p1 across row
When you reach what WOULD be the 15th(16th,17th) row k1, p1 (the texture makes the counting easy), instead of doing the k1, p1, work a garter stitch band by knitting the next 6 rows, and then, with a wrong side row about to be worked, follow the chart for your size.
   When charted design is completed, knit 8 rows, and then bind off purlwise. Break yarn off, leaving a 20" length of yarn still attached to the knitting to simplify sewing later.

FRONT
Work exactly as for the back until the third center diamond of the yoke has just been completed. (The next row to be worked will be a right side row.) Keeping in pattern, work 31(34,37) sts; bind off center 19 sts purlwise; work remaining 31(34,37) sts.

Working on one shoulder at a time, bind off 1 st (slip 1, work 1, pass slipped st over: this is a PSSO) at neck edge every other row 5 times. Complete chart and garter band to correspond with back, and then repeat precess with other shoulder.

Press wrong side of work lightly, measuring carefully as you do so to ensure that pieces are of the correct dimensions. A real advantage of using good wool is that you can coax your work into shape easily, without damaging it! Make sure selvedges are nice and smooth to ensure easy sewing later.

SHOULDER SEAMS
Place front and back pieces together, right sides facing. The bound-off edges will seem slightly beveled towards each other: sew the seams by catching the upper loops of the bound off sts using the length of yarn previously left attached. This will create an attractive finish in which the join itself is virtually invisible from the right side of the work.

SLEEVES
Working from the right side of the work, beginning about 2" above the yoke's garter st band, pick up 73 sts... this is about 3 sts for every 4 rows of work. K 6 rows, and then complete diamond design from sleeve chart. Purl the next 6 rows, decreasing 1 st at the start of each of these rows (again, sl 1, work 1, PSSO), 67 sts rem.

Establish the same pattern as for the body:
   Row 1: K, Row 2: P, Row 3: K,
   Row 4: K1, p1 across row

After working these 4 rows once with no decreases, begin to shape sleeve by slipping the first st of each row 1 and row 2, and working the 2nd st before passing the slipped st over it. Continue this until 39(41,43) sts remain. When sleeve measures 15(15^1/$_2$, 15^1/$_2$)" from start of garter ridges – or as desired, minus cuff – switch to smaller needles and begin cuff on what would be a row 4 of the pattern sequence. K1, p1 rib for 3" and then bind off in ribbing (knit the k sts, and purl the p sts as you come to them, before binding them off). Break yarn off, leaving a 20" length attached for sewing.

SEAMS
Again, press work lightly from wrong side. Sew side and underarm seams together, and work in any ends of yarn there might be.

NECK
With circular needle, pick up approx 76 - 80 sts from right side of work, beginning at back right shoulder. Work 5 rows of k1, p1 rib before binding off in ribbing. Weave in end, and press lightly again.

Cables and Diamonds

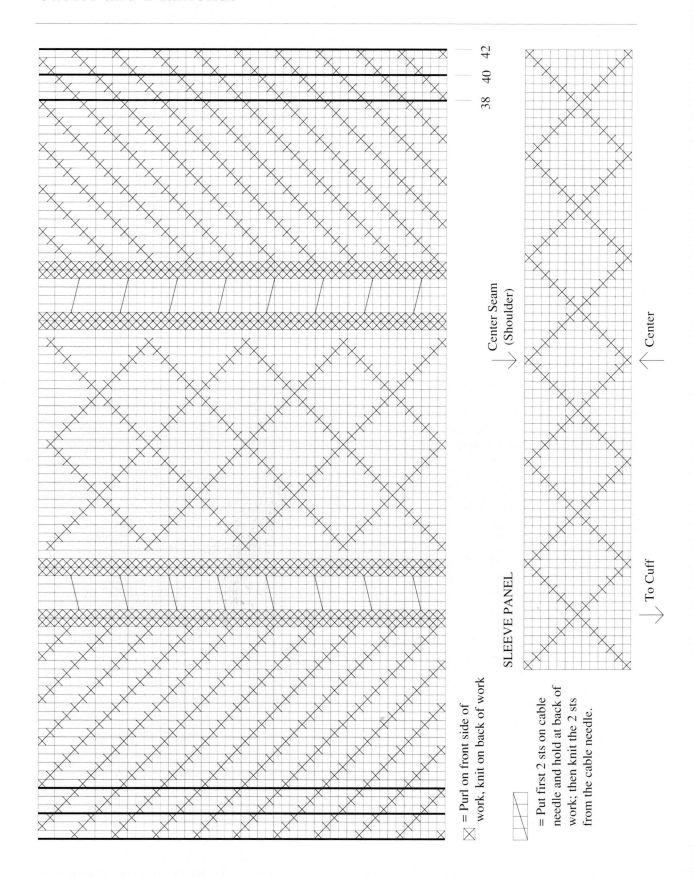

38 40 42

Center Seam
(Shoulder)

Center

SLEEVE PANEL

To Cuff

⊠ = Purl on front side of
work, knit on back of work

= Put first 2 sts on cable
needle and hold at back of
work; then knit the 2 sts
from the cable needle.

Peg Richard

Peg Richard has found socks to be a recurring focus of her artistic life, and they were our introduction to each other. I had seen an article by Peg in *Threads* magazine and was taken with the wonderful multicolored Fair Isle knicker socks pictured. When I read that the designer lived in Maine, I was determined to meet her.

We did get together one afternoon, in her second-floor apartment in Portland, Maine's largest city. Soon after I arrived, she pulled out not just socks, but numerous sweaters rich with the aroma of her cedar chest, and I could see that this was a woman with a passion for Fair Isle. She had baby sweaters, adult cardigans, and even a stunning vest she had made for her husband to wear to a job interview. ("People remember you if you wear a nice sweater." Good idea!)

Peg was raised in a snowy western Maine town in a home where knitting was abundant. A home that was "filled with the winter smells of wet socks drying on the radiators." Her very resourceful mother was always creating sweaters, socks, hats, and mittens for her seven children, and she continues the knitting tradition by creating 30 pairs of mittens every year for a Santa's helper project. Many of the yarns her mother used were hearty wools from Canadian mills, which created long-lasting garments. Neighbors would often pass on old sweaters to her so she could unravel them and reuse the yarn, often re-dying it. Peg can remember the thrill, as a young girl, of having something knit for her from yarn taken from a sweater that once belonged to an admired neighborhood teenager. She also remembers her father, who worked in a paper mill, bringing home discarded wool felts, which are used as a cushion during the papermaking process, and her resourceful family even found ways to reuse that wool.

Peg worked as a costume maker in Boston, creating costumes for Boston Ballet productions such as "Swan Lake." She tired of the muted fabric colors she worked with in this and other Victorian productions, and she began knitting brightly colored socks on the subway to relieve the boredom. Socks were a perfect project because they only needed small amounts of yarn and hence were very portable. She eventually moved on to a job at the Radcliffe College offices, where a pictured selection of her socks decorated the school Christmas card, and some of her knit bathing suits were used for another card cover and an ad. Knitting socks became a business when the owner of a "sock cart" in Fanueil Hall, Boston's busy shopping area, saw the card and asked to sell her socks. The socks were in big demand but Peg found it hard to make a profit knitting these involved patterns.

After working at many different jobs to set aside three years' savings, Peg and her husband, Rob, set off on a 13-month bike tour of Europe. Trying to travel with as few possessions as possible, Peg thought she could leave her knitting at home, but soon realized that it was a part of her life she couldn't be without. As they moved slowly through the small towns and big cities, Peg found that knitting was a great introduction to strangers. People would often come up to talk as she sat knitting in cafés or on park benches. Occasionally Peg and Rob would be invited to spend the night in the homes of

Peg Richard

people whose introduction to Peg and Rob had been through her knitting. As they entered a new country, the first word she would learn in the language was "yarn," and Rob knew enough to pull out a book and prepare for a stop whenever she spotted a yarn shop.

Peg, now the mother of a two-year-old daughter, continues to pursue her craft while working part time as a school art teacher. She works in a neighborhood school and often incorporates fiber arts into her classes, including Navaho weaving. She also has plans to start a garden of plants used for dyeing as part of the school's new nature trail and hopes to introduce natural dyeing and spinning to her classes.

Peg keeps a sketchbook of ideas and adds new Fair Isle patterns whenever she sees one that interests her or a new idea comes into her mind. As they traveled throughout Europe, she saw many wonderful patterns and occasionally she would sketch patterns in her book from sweaters people were wearing. She keeps note cards and drawings and anything that may at some point inspire her to create a pattern. Very old traditional patterns, such as those from Lapland, intrigue her.

Peg has a degree in art, and she draws on some of her educational experiences to create her patterns, particularly using rules and theories of colors. She recommends "color opposites to create vibrant combinations" and often finds that a color that at first doesn't seem right, "may actually become an asset to the design."

Like most knitters, she can't imagine not having a project to pick up whenever she sits down, and she often knits on her lunch hour at work. This often turns into an impromptu teaching/learning experience for those around her, something Peg loves.

As we talked, Peg mentioned how often socks reappear in her life, even though she occasionally stops knitting them for periods of time and prefers creating sweaters. On a cold night last winter there was a fire on her street, and a neighboring family suddenly was out on the street in their nightclothes. Rob remembered an old box of handmade socks Peg had stashed away, and he rushed to retrieve it. As he walked over to offer the neighbors some warm wool socks, Peg realized that socks were always going to be part of her life.

Fair Isle and Baby Socks

Fair Isle Socks

Size: Medium

Needles: Four size 3 double-pointed needles, 7-8 in. lengths to obtain gauge size of 7 sts and $7^1/_2$ rows = 1 in. Size is medium. Blunt tapestry needle.

Materials: Four oz. sport-weight plum (MC), one oz. each gold, medium gold, orange, royal blue and jade green. I used Brown Sheep Company single-ply sport weight yarn and Christopher Farm single ply yarn. The medium-gold and orange yarns are fine weaving yarns, color blended by working two strands together.

KNITTING DIRECTIONS

With MC, cast on 84 sts and divide on three needles. Work one rnd k1, p1 rib. Then work k1, p1 corrugated rib in main color and orange shading to gold for $1^1/_2$ in. Knit MC for four rnds. Begin pattern as shown in chart 1. Work until $6^1/_2$ in. from beg or desired length to widest part of calf. Continuing in pattern, dec 2 sts every 4th rnd six times as follows: at beginning of rnd, k2tog; work in pattern to last 3 sts of rnd and sl 1-k1-psso or ssk; k1 (last st of rnd)-72 sts. Continue in pattern until sock measures $15^1/_2$" or desired length to ankle.

HEEL

Place 36 sts on one needle for heel; center st is last st of rnd. Work in MC: Row 1 (RS): *Sl 1, k1, *repeat *-* to end. Row 2 (WS): Purl. For a deep heel counter work these two rows until flap is as long as it is wide; or work as many rows as stitches for a shallow counter.

GUSSET DECREASE

When heel is done, pick up sts for gussets. Decrease on the three sts next to the instep, as you knit around the foot, until same number of sts as at the ankle remain. With heavier yarns, decrease every round; with fingering or light sport yarns, decrease every other round as follows: On 3 sts before

Chart 1

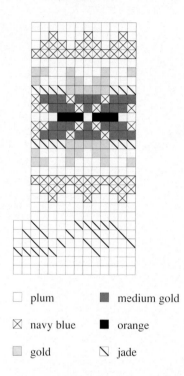

□ plum	▨ medium gold
⊠ navy blue	■ orange
▨ gold	◹ jade

Seed Pattern

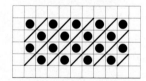

instep: Sl 1-k1-psso or ssk, k1; on 3 sts after instep k1, k2tog. Work until 72 sts remain. Work foot using seed pattern for the sole and the fair isle pattern on top.

TOE

When 2 in. from end of foot, using MC only, decrease 4 sts on each decrease round-every round for heavier yarn; every other round for lighter yarn as follows: On the last 3 sts of the sole and instep, sl 1-k1-psso or ssk, k1; on the first 3 sts of the instep and sole, k1, k2tog. For a shorter toe, plan any number of decreases (k2tog) evenly spaced around the toe for the number of rounds desired. Graft last 6 toe sts together.

Socks for Babies

Fair isle socks are perfect for infants. Besides being warm, fair isle designs can help a sock stay on a plump foot in constant motion. Because they don't receive hard wear, socks for babies can be made from more softly spun yarns. Generally, the longer the sock, the more likely it is to stay on a baby and grow with the child.

For quickly growing children, I rely upon an old standard – the spiral knit sock. It acts as a tube sock, hugging the foot and creating its own heel. Adding a multicolored cuff, modeled after turn-of-the-century golf hose, not only gives extra warmth and color, but helps the socks to stay on. To knit a spiral sock, cast on a multiple of six stitches. Work in k1, p1 for four rows, k a multicolored cuff for 2-3 inches, and turn the cuff inside out k1 p1 etc. and then begin spiral rib. To work spiral rib, k3, p3 for 3 rows. Every 4th row, move rib over one stitch, for example p1, k3, p2. When sock is the desired length finish with a normal toe by dividing sts evenly onto two needles. At beg of row *k1, sl 1, psso, k to last two sts on needle k2tog. Repeat this twice each round. Work until 3 sts on each needle. Break off yarn and draw through sts. Fasten on inside and weave in end.

Cuff Chart

☐ pink

■ spruce

■ burgundy

▨ cream

⊠ medium gold

Portions of this pattern were first published in *Threads* magazine.

Marty Tracy—Peace Fleece

When I first called the Soviet American Woolen Company and heard the message on their answering machine, I was startled to realize it was repeated both in English and Russian. I was struck by the image of a Russian person calling this small Maine town to ask a question of Peter or Marty in just the way I had picked up the phone and dialed. Eventually, I realized that this is a clue to goals of the venture — that through business, Soviet American Woolens was attempting to compel us to see that although we may be individuals who were living in cultures with great geographic and political differences, we were still very similar people who might actually use our phones to dial the same number.

Marty Tracy and her husband Peter Hagerty are creators of yarn, sweaters, knitting kits, and more — they are attempting to improve the prospects for international peace. They took up sheep farming in the early seventies and struggled with the low return from selling lamb and fleeces, realizing that they needed to create a product that could add value to these raw materials. This economic need, coupled with a serious concern about the future harmony of the world combined to create their product, Peace Fleece.

Peter, who has a degree in psychology, had been supplementing their income with shearing and logging. Marty was trained at the Boston Museum School, and after moving to their western Maine farm, she began working as a potter, producing beautiful blue and white hand-painted creations. Her work was very popular and always sold out quickly at fairs and to wholesalers. She had been at this trade for twelve years when she and Peter developed the idea for Peace Fleece. One year Marty had gotten involved with a summer work camp that brought thirteen European students to their area to participate in community projects. This process "internationalized me," says Marty, and began to give her a sense of a diverse world far beyond the bounds of the rural community where they had settled.

This experience increased Marty's and Peter's concerns about the nuclear threat and the growing disharmony in the world. After Peter watched "The Day After," a television movie that dealt with the staggering aftereffects of a nuclear war, they began to think about how they could make a contribution to improving the prospects for world peace.

Together, Peter and Marty conceived of the idea of blending Soviet and American fleece to create a yarn that they could sell in both countries. They called their company Soviet American Woolens and their product Peace Fleece. Peter traveled to Russia in 1985, long before trade opened up, and was able to negotiate a deal for 1200 pounds of wool. He and Marty had this wool spun by the Harrisville Mill in New Hampshire and named the colors such things as Negotiation Gray, Lenin Lime, Soyuz-Apollo Blue and Borsht. They packaged some of the yarns as sweater kits, using Soviet themes as their motifs.

At this point, Marty was still creating her pottery full-time, but she soon decided to direct all of her attention to their new venture. Although she had been very successful as a potter, Marty felt that she was ready to make a change from the isolated life of an artist to the more sociable world of running the business. She now feels that this has been a great choice both for herself and her family. She and Peter share the chores of the business, each taking on different tasks. On the brochure, for instance, Marty does the wonderful graphics and Peter contributes the copy, often discussing the return trips he has made to Russia to show others some of the things he has experienced.

Marty knits, and although she doesn't design all of the company's sweaters, she did do the one in this book, with the help of Hélène Rush. Marty said this pattern was one that had been in her mind for years, and because of that, it was down on paper in fifteen minutes. Other kit designs have come from several designers, including a Russian woman.

Over the years they have expanded their product line to include other creations imported from Russia through a venture they call Familyworks — a project jointly managed by Soviet American Woolens and a Moscow Cooperative. They manufacture wooden knitting needles, milled in Maine and then shipped to the Soviet Union where the end balls are painted in bright colors by the Soviet students. These are sold in a beautiful paper pouch covered with Marty's stunning graphics. They also sell hand-painted wooden buttons and cobalt blue porcelain sheep created by the students — each one is different. Their kits and products are sold through yarn shops, in mail-order catalogues, and through their own newsletters and brochures.

The company has grown steadily over the years, helped by considerable media attention to their unique idea. Along with selling their growing line of products, Peter has led yearly trips to the USSR and co-sponsored an April Wool festival there. Unfortunately, due to the unstable political conditions as well as the lack of food and medical supplies, the 1991 trip was canceled. In 1990, for the first time, Marty and their two children traveled along with Peter to the Soviet Union. It was a very moving experience for the whole family, and all

Marty Tracy, a Russian friend, and her daughter Cora Hagerty

returned with strong memories of the people who had become part of their lives for the past years. In 1990, a group of eight students, two parents, and two Soviet TV reporters came to the United States to set up a booth at the Common Ground Country Fair, a popular Maine attraction, where they had tremendous success selling their crafts.

What's next for this creative family? Since Marty and Peter's goal is finding ways to involve people from conflicting cultures in business ventures, they are now looking into the possibility of developing products that would encourage Israelis and Palestinians to work together. The recent political and economic upheavals in the former Soviet republics will continue to affect their business, of course, but Peter expresses his strong commitment to creating products that will, at least in a small way, help bring harmony to a disharmonious world.

Peace Fleece
Woman's Cardigan

Sizes: 32(34,36,38,40)"
Finished Sizes: 35(37,39,41,43)"
Needles: Size 4 and 6 needles to obtain
   stitch gauge of 4.5 sts = 1" in solid color
   and stitch gauge of 5 sts = 1" in color
   pattern.
Materials:
   4 4 oz skeins A
   3 4 oz skeins B
   $1/2$ 4 oz skein C
   8 buttons

STITCHES USED
Stockinette Stitch (St st): K1 row, p1 row.
Seed Stitch: Row 1: K1, p1. Row 2: K on p,
p on k.

BACK
With smaller needles and B cast on
80(86,90,96,100) sts. Work in k1, p1 rib for
3", inc 5 sts evenly in last row –
85(91,95,101,105) sts. Then, with larger
needles and working in St st, work Chart 1
repeating these 14 rows. At 13(13$1/2$,14,
14$1/2$ 15)" from beginning, SHAPE ARM-
HOLE: Keeping color pattern as established,
bind off 5 sts at beg of next 2 rows, then dec
1 st each end every other row 5 times. Work
even on remaining 65(71,75,81,85) sts until
4" above armhole ending with a solid row A
on chart. Then, with smaller needles, work
stripe pattern for rest of back as follows: 2
rows B, 2 rows A. Work even until 7$1/4$(7$1/2$,
8,8$1/4$,8$1/2$)" above armhole. Right side
facing, bind off 19(22,23,26,27) sts, leave
next 27(27,29,29,31) sts on holder for back
of neck, bind off remaining sts.

LEFT FRONT
With smaller needles and B, cast on
40(42,44,48,50) sts. Work in k1, p1 rib inc
3(4,4,3,3) sts evenly in last row –
43(46,48,51,53) sts. Then, with larger
needles, and working in St st, work Chart 1
repeating as needed and shaping armhole as
for back where required. Once shaping is
complete, ending with a solid row A and
right side facing, work Chart 2 on these
33(36,38,41,43) sts for 12 rows, work 2 rows
A, then with smaller needles, in stripe
pattern as for back for rest of front. AT
THE SAME TIME, at 5$1/4$(5$1/2$,6,6$1/4$,6$1/2$)"
above armhole, SHAPE NECK: Leave
11(11,12,12,13) sts on holder at neck edge,
then dec1 st at same edge every other row 3
times. Work even on remaining
19(22,23,26,27) sts until same length as
back to shoulder. Bind off all sts.

RIGHT FRONT
Work as for left front reversing shaping.

SLEEVES
With smaller needles and B, cast on
40(42,42,44,44) sts. Work in k1, p1 rib for
3" inc 19 sts evenly in last row -
59(61,61,63,63) sts. Then, with larger
needles and working in St st work in pattern
as follows: 12 rows A, 1 row B, 1 row C, 1
row B. Repeat these 15 rows to armhole.
AT THE SAME TIME, inc 1 st each end
every 2$1/4$2$1/3$,2$1/3$,2$1/2$, 2$1/2$)" 6 times -
71(73,73,75,75) sts. At 17(17$1/2$,18,18$1/2$,
19)" from beg, SHAPE ARMHOLE AND
CAP: Working with B only for rest of
sleeve, bind off 5 sts at beg of next 2 rows,
then dec 1 st each end every other row until
25 sts remain. Bind off 2 sts at beg of next 8
rows. Bind off remaining 9 sts.

NECKBAND

Sew shoulder seams. With smaller needles and B, work across 11(11,12,12,13) sts from right front holder, pick-up and k 12 sts on side of neck, work across 27(27,29,29,31) sts from back holder, pick-up and k 12 sts on side of neck, work across 11(11,12,12,13) sts from left front holder. Work back and forth on these 73(73,77,77,81) sts in Seed Stitch for 1". Bind off all sts.

LEFT BAND

With smaller needles and B, pick-up and k 96 (100,104,110,112) sts on front edge. Work in Seed Stitch for 1". Bind off all sts.

RIGHT BUTTONHOLE BAND

Work as for left one for $\frac{1}{2}$". Right side facing, work as follows: work on 2(4,2,2,3) sts, [yo, k2 tog, work on 11(11,12,13,13) sts] 7 times, yo, k2 tog, work on 1(3,2,1,2) sts. Work even until band is 1" wide. Bind off all sts.

FINISHING

Sew buttons opposite buttonholes. Set in sleeves at armhole. Sew underarm and side seams.

CHART 1

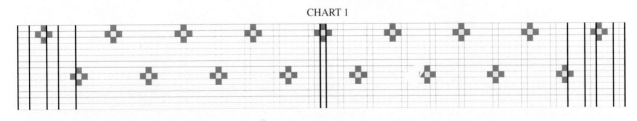

40 38   36 34   32   Work to here for front.   32   34 36   38 40

CHART 2

☐ A
■ B
☐ C

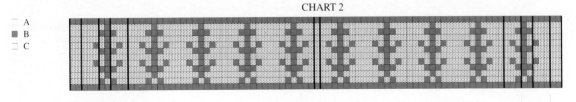

40 38   36 34   32   Work to here for center front.   32   34 36   38 40

Peace Fleece Woman's Cardigan

About Our Models

Once again, while doing this book, Peter Ralston (the photographer) and I have been blessed with many wonderful people who willingly allow us to drag them around looking for the right spot to take their photo. We do this on cold days and warm, walking through the last of the snow with cold, wet feet or sweating in the hot sun in wool sweaters. As with our other three books, in this one all of the models are local people. Some have spent their lives here in the community; others are "from away," but have recently moved here or spend the summer with us.

Jessie, our cover model, is the third member of the same family to grace our covers. Her father is the principal of our sixty-five student school and her step-mother, Christie, was on the cover of the last book, *Sweaters from the Maine Islands*. Jessie is a student at a Maine college and comes back in the summers to teach swimming and work on a landscaping crew. Jessie's older sister, Amanda, who was on the cover of *Maine Island Classics*, appears on page 78. Amanda is outgoing and adventuresome and spent part of the last year studying at sea and visiting such exotic places as the Malaysia and Japan. Amanda is lively and fun, and their home is never dull when she is around.

Monica, on page 55, is my daughter's best friend. One of the joys of small-town life is that you know all of your children's friends along with the friend's siblings, parents, and relatives. Her mother and I are good friends, and her father is the captain of our ferry. Monica has lived here all of her life and I have had the privilege of watching her grow into a very beautiful and articulate fifteen-year-old.

My daughter Hannah, Monica's constant companion, is pictured on page 66. Hannah has lived here all of her life as well, and she has benefited greatly from the safe yet challenging existence island life provides. She is one of a class of five in her high school, so there is no lack of attention from her teachers. She has developed a strong sense of being a member of a community from growing up in a town where everyone's voice can be heard. She spends her summers on the water teaching sailing, and like all of the kids, she can ride her bike anywhere she wants to go.

We photographed a wonderful team of three sisters in our children's sweaters. Lindsey (page 58), April (page 27) and Alicia were all very patient as we moved from one flower bed to the next looking for the perfect backdrop. Alicia, at age 3, turned out to be a little too small, but we had fun with her anyway, and her two big sisters

About Our Models

were perfect models, smiling warmly on cue.

On page 40 you'll see Allison, with the beautiful eyes, who has willingly posed for us several times. Now the mother of three children all under eight, Allison is a hard worker. She and her husband live in a village house, with the world's smallest vegetable garden right next to the road. Their house is always a beehive of activity with neighborhood kids playing in their yard. They have a very special son, James, who is autistic and a real favorite of the community, especially when he gets up and reads at the Christmas plays or other school performances.

From the first book to this fourth, we have always tried to catch Angela (page 15), when we could, to appear in our photo-graphs. We were fortunate this summer as Angela, an art school graduate, was back on the island working in a gallery and preparing for a show of her hand painted furniture. Angela has a great sense of humor and always manages to keep us entertained while we work.

Barb (page 79, left), is the sister of Carol — one of our crew. She is also an art student and spends the summer with her sister, taking on jobs of every sort including working for us when she can squeeze it in. Barb is a wonderful model and it is never hard to get her to smile. Linda, on page 41, was a kindergarten/first grade teacher. She has now gone on to teaching in New Hampshire, but was much loved during the two years she taught here. Her classroom was always busy and filled with happy students.

Sources of Supply

If you cannot find the materials locally to make the sweaters in this book, they are almost all available through North Island Designs. We sell kits, skeined yarns, and yarn packs (all of the yarns needed to create one of these designs packaged together in just the right quantities). We also have a catalog of many knitting kits not in this book as well as accessories such as buttons and wooden knitting needles, and our three other pattern books. You can call us toll free to place an order, to ask a knitting question, or just to check on our weather. If you add your name to our mailing list, you will receive our newsletter — keeping you updated on our new designs and stories of island life.

Some of the kits and yarns discussed in the book are available through us, or you may contact these businesses directly.

North Island Designs
Main Street
North Haven, Maine 04853
1-800-548-5648
207-867-4788 (Maine and Canada)

S. M. Hanson Designs
Susie Hanson
18 Avon Ave.
York, Maine 03909
207-363-8083
Christmas Stocking kits and children's sweaters

Soviet American Woolens
RFD 1, Box 57
Kezar Falls, Maine 04047
207-625-4906
"Peace Fleece" yarns, kits, knitted goods and accessories

Swans Island Farm
Carol Loehr
Box R
Atlantic, Maine 04608
207-526-4435
Yarn and kits

NORTH ISLAND DESIGNS
INCORPORATED

You may contact us directly if you are unable to find any of the materials we have recommended in the book. We have kits, yarn packs (a kit without the pattern) and skeined yarns. We are also here to answer your knitting questions and you can reach us through our toll free number.

If you would like our color brochure or yarn sample cards ($7 ppd) just call or send us one of these postpaid cards. Once your name is on our mailing list, you will receive our quarterly newsletter with descriptions of our latest designs as well as news from the island.

Call our toll free number:
1-800-548-5648
Or in Maine:
1-867-4788
Or send in one of the attached cards.

To Order Books:
Send in the card opposite to order any of our titles.

Since this card goes to a different address, be sure to send in one of the top cards to place your name on *our* mailing list.

To receive a free Down East catalog of fine books and gifts, call **207-594-9544** or **1-800-766-1670**.

Please Send Me . . . *Your Catalog and Price List.*

Name_____

Street Address_____

Town_____ State_____ Zip_____

. . . Add a friend to your mailing list!

Name_____

Street Address_____

Town_____ State_____ Zip_____

Phone Orders: 1-800-548-5648 In Maine 1-867-4788

CB

. . . Here are some friends *for your mailing list!*

Name_____

Street Address_____

Town_____ State_____ Zip_____

Name_____

Street Address_____

Town_____ State_____ Zip_____

CB

Down East Books
P.O. Box 679, Camden, Maine 04843

ORDER FORM

Quantity	Item	Price	Total
	1 — Maine Island Classics	**$15.95**	
	2 — Maine Island Kids	**$15.95**	
	3 — Sweaters from the Maine Islands	**$16.95**	
	4 — North Island Designs 4	**$17.95**	

METHOD OF PAYMENT

Mastercard_____ Visa_____ Check_____

Acct. #_____ Exp. Date_____

Signature_____

Name_____

Address_____

_____ Tel._____

Subtotal _____
Me. Res. 6% Sales Tax _____
Shipping* _____
TOTAL _____

*Add $3.25 for first book, $1.00 for each additional book. We ship UPS unless you specify otherwise.

BUSINESS REPLY MAIL
FIRST CLASS   PERMIT NO. 1   NORTH HAVEN, MAINE

POSTAGE WILL BE PAID BY ADDRESSEE

NO POSTAGE
NECESSARY
IF MAILED
IN THE
UNITED STATES

North Island Designs
Main Street
North Haven, ME
04853

BUSINESS REPLY MAIL
FIRST CLASS   PERMIT NO. 1   NORTH HAVEN, MAINE

POSTAGE WILL BE PAID BY ADDRESSEE

NO POSTAGE
NECESSARY
IF MAILED
IN THE
UNITED STATES

North Island Designs
Main Street
North Haven, ME
04853

PLEASE ENCLOSE THIS ORDER FORM
(WITH PAYMENT, IF PAYING BY CHECK)
IN AN ENVELOPE AND
RETURN TO:

Down East Books
P.O. Box 679, Camden, Maine 04843